The Blue Ridge

Text and Photographs by

WILLIAM A. BAKE

LIBRARY
CALDWELL COMMUNITY COLLEGE
HUDSON, NC

OXMOOR HOUSE, INC.
Birmingham

D1299731

THE BLUE RIDGE

Copyright © by William A. Bake, 1977

First published in hardback in 1977 by The Viking Press

Published in 1984 by Oxmoor House, Inc.,
Book Division of Southern Progress Corporation
Post Office Box 2463
Birmingham, Alabama 35201

9505

ALL RIGHTS RESERVED.

95-96

No part of this book may be reproduced in any form or by any means without the prior written permission of the Publisher, excepting brief quotes in connection with reviews written specifically for inclusion in a magazine or newspaper.

Library of Congress Catalog Number: 83-61839

ISBN: 0-8487-0631-5

Printed in the United States of America

Cover and title page design by:
Design for Publishing, Bob and Faith Nance
Homewood, Alabama

Contents

To Claudia:
   through whose
     beauty
      I
        see the world

Preface

In the reality of human experience, places have little meaning apart from people. The Blue Ridge Mountains, like all places, exist on two levels: physical and experiential. The peaks have their physical dimensions and the life upon them can be categorized, but little identification with the mountains is possible until they have been experienced. These are mountains of antiquity, green wilderness, and powerful rivers. The impact of these Appalachian aspects on people has been, and continues to be, profound. Generations of mountain people evolved a way of living that we in many respects admire today. Present generations find personal but shared experiences in these mountains that bring satisfaction to their lives. We are not impartial toward the Blue Ridge Mountains; they are too much a part of us. Mountains are what I write of, then, but in a deeper sense this is a book about human experience.

Prologue: Dawn Flight

The Boeing 727 caught the first rays of the rising sun just as it left the runway. Pulling forward against the force of the climb, I glanced out the window and then watched as a shadow slowly worked its way across the wing. The Southern Piedmont, deceptively flat from even the slightest altitude, dropped away into a random array of piny woods, highways, and subdivisions. Climbing through three thousand feet on a dawn flight from Atlanta, Georgia, to Washington, D.C., we turned, allowing me a brief glimpse of Stone Mountain, an ancient domelike monadnock near Atlanta now set aglow by the orange light of the early morning sun. To the east, the Piedmont lay hidden beneath an endless sea of low clouds. Satisfied that there would be nothing to see, I settled back.

Still climbing, the plane banked slightly, causing a sharp ray of sunlight to cut in through a window across the aisle. Bothered by the brightness, I looked out again. The cloud mass ended abruptly at the Blue Ridge. From a modest beginning near our position northwest of Gainesville, Georgia, the ridge was beginning to rise to elevations that would put its frontal scarp as much as twenty-five hundred feet directly above the Southern Piedmont, near Blowing Rock, North Carolina. Not until it stretched some five hundred and fifty miles northeast to its terminus near Carlisle, Pennsylvania, would the Blue Ridge end.

The plane was reaching toward a cruising altitude of thirty-three thousand feet—too high for anything but the more general land features to show. Yet I could clearly see where the Blue Ridge ended abruptly as its tumbled peaks gave way to the parallel ridges and valleys of Tennessee west of Chattanooga. Then, for a few moments, the Great Valley, a geologic feature extending along the western ramparts of the Blue Ridge, lay below. Here called the Tennessee Valley, it bears other names to the north—the Shenandoah and Cumberland among them. Passing over Pulaski and then Gordonville, Tennessee, in an air route firmly inscribed on the charts and scopes of the Federal Aviation Administration, we curved gently back east toward Washington.

South of us were ranges with names enshrined in American folklore, and mountains with names known to few but those living along their slopes: the Snowbirds, the Nantahalas, the Cohuttas, and the Great Smokies, the Balsams, and the Pisgah—ranges too numerous to mention. And peaks—forty-six of them topping six thousand feet—whose names roll off the tongue like a litany in Cherokee and a primer in Scotch-

Irish: Yonah, Cheoah, Wayah, Tanasee, and Unicoi. Dog Loser Knob, Nobreeches Ridge, Pumpkin Patch Mountain, and Rough Butt Bald. This was the southern Blue Ridge, a geologic province that includes all the mountains between the Southern Piedmont and Great Valley or, if you prefer it, an area that is defined as the eastern front range of the Southern Appalachians from Georgia to Pennsylvania. Whatever the area, these mountains are botanically, geologically, and culturally one. Accepting that as a guideline, these pages deal principally with the eastern ranges but occasionally mention such mountains as the more westerly Great Smokies and Iron Range.

At the latitude of Asheville, North Carolina, the Blue Ridge is eighty miles wide, with many outliers in the Piedmont to the southeast; northward it narrows drastically until, north of Roanoke, Virginia, the main ridge does not exceed fourteen miles in width or rise more than a fraction above four thousand feet. Near the point where the Blue Ridge begins to narrow northward, we again crossed it. To the southwest, the mountains tumbled haphazardly to the horizon, but northeastward lay only a few parallel ridges with smaller spurs extending from them. The names were fewer now too: South Mountain, Short Hill, the Catoctin and Bull Run mountains, and the Carlisle Prong pretty well complete the list. From an airliner, and often from the ridges themselves, it would be possible to see the entire width of the northern Blue Ridge.

In those portions of the Great Valley that lie west of the northern Blue Ridge, great rivers rise and flow east through the mountains into the Atlantic. Through great rends in the rocks called water gaps, the Roanoke, the James, and then, the biggest and best known, the Potomac, breach the Blue Ridge. Notching the ridges in other places are less pronounced gaps known as wind gaps. Three of them—Manassas, Ashby, and Snickers gaps in Virginia—are especially prominent. In geologically ancient times streams flowed in them eastward from the mountains, beginning a downcutting action and then ceasing their flow.

The flight was now over the Piedmont and the densely populated Baltimore-Washington area. Without any apparent change in the land below, we descended over the Coastal Plain and followed the sluggish Potomac toward Washington. The Coastal Plain is historically the oldest settled land in the white man's America. In history as well as geography, the mountains stand in counterposition to this low country. Too high, too rugged, and too forested, they were for a hundred and fifty years a barrier beyond which settlement was only temporary. Yet by the 1750s and 1760s Scotch-Irish and German pioneers were moving along them southward from Pennsylvania and northwestward from Charleston, South Carolina. By the time of the Revolution they had thinly settled the Piedmont and occupied a few valleys in the Blue Ridge.

Almost from the beginning the southern mountaineers were thought to be backward. At the least, they were an independent lot, willing to fight Crown loyalists and Cherokee Indians, to stay loyal to the Union during the Civil War, and to outwit federal revenue agents during Prohibition. Being isolated from the low country by both topography and sheer distance, they also developed independence in the practicalities of daily living. From the land, they gathered and sold cash crops, such as chestnuts and ginseng. In their clearings they planted corn, potatoes, and apples, and raised pigs and cattle. Through the decades their habits

7

persisted, causing the rest of the nation at first to laugh at them and then to recognize a certain richness in their folkways. Today Appalachian arts and crafts are among the most celebrated in the country.

Impoverished in terms of material wealth, the people of the Blue Ridge depended on the natural bounty of their land. When finally poor farming practices and outside lumbering combined to rob the mountains of their richness, the Blue Ridge mountaineer was left with little but his beliefs and the memories that had given them birth. Today there is a melancholy look to this land that is reflected in the faces of its people and heard in their music and speech. Weathered buildings blend with the woods, and fields of wind-blown broom sedge flicker in the evening sunlight. Parks, wilderness areas, and abandoned farms cover vast tracts of land that once were logged and farmed and have since eroded. This is good country again, both savage and gentle, grand and subtle—country given to life.

Within a few moments the excitement and challenge of Washington would be at hand. In the next few days the course of my life would be changed. A new career and a move from Georgia to West Virginia were in the making. Years of exploring the Georgia and Carolina portion of the Blue Ridge were about to end, but in the years to follow I would come to know these mountains in Virginia, West Virginia, and Maryland. My impression of them would not be altered by the experience, for in their natural aspects the Blue Ridge Mountains are for the most part a unity. But, as I would soon come to realize, I was moving into a border region. In Maryland the cultural heritage differs sharply from that of the South.

With good cause the Indians called the Blue Ridge "the unending mountains." Passing seasons rich with experience have made them seem so to me. I have spent much time exploring these peaks, yet in retrospect I have seen only a representative sampling of them. Even if a man could see them all and meet their people, with the experience behind him, he might yet see new frontiers in them. Beyond their physical dimensions lies something spiritual. They speak of the past and its continuity with us. The memories, if not the mountains, are endless.

Southern Sentinels

Midway between the first tentative beginnings of the Blue Ridge in north Georgia and the highest peaks in the Great Smoky Mountains, the crest of 4784-foot Brasstown Bald Mountain commands a view of the Blue Ridge that is limited only by the haze. One especially clear day I stood in the fire tower that projects turret-like above the U.S. Forest Service visitor center there. Merely by turning around, I could see Stone Mountain, Georgia, to the south and then Clingmans Dome, on the Tennessee–North Carolina line. Though the difference in elevation between the crests of the two mountains is about five thousand feet, neither commanded more than a fraction of the horizon. Height is not the measure of these mountains. Their true dimension is their extension into time.

Particularly is this true of the ancient granite exposures just southeast of the Blue Ridge. Strictly speaking, the granite exposures are a part of the Southern Piedmont, not the Blue Ridge. In both geology and botany they are distinctive, sharing little with most of the mountains just to the north. Yet they are in a sense preludes—or sentinels, if you will. Upon seeing Stone Mountain, the first high landform to break the horizon from the south, one has every expectation of seeing more mountains beyond—and is soon satisfied in that respect. Visually, they are the first of the southern mountains, deserving, in their own way, of mention as preludes to the Blue Ridge.

Each of these exposures represents a surfacing of a vast Precambrian pavement of igneous and metamorphic rock that underlies the Southeast beneath the Blue Ridge and Piedmont. And each is a worn remnant of mountains even more ancient in their unchanged appearance than the Southern Appalachians of today. On all of them, plant cover is sparse and the granite dominates. The exposures are generally low, sometimes even flat, and they begin absolutely abruptly and often without warning. Of the many I have visited, most are so unannounced by any changes in topography that one must have precise directions to locate them. Only the high granite monadnocks of DeKalb County, Georgia, east of Atlanta, announce themselves from any distance. But all of them are completely at odds with the piny-woods-and-old-fields aspect of the upper Piedmont. Undulating and bulging, they are waterworn expanses of gray granite, ancient and unyielding.

Stone Mountain, the largest and best known of them, is a brooding 1683-foot hulk. Wearing only scattered patches of soil, it looks like a giant epidermal wart on the earth's surface. Scattered across its slopes like sloughed-off scales are slabs of granite. Exfoliation, the geologists call this process of slabbing. Water seeps into cracks in the granite, freezes and expands to split the rock, or relentlessly dissolves minute fragments of granite, finally splitting off the slabs. Where the slopes are gentle, the slabs lie scattered across the granite, but along the bases of cliffs, huge jumbles of rock lie heaped and hidden by forest growth. Amid the rock slabs, gnarled trees eke out an existence, and occasionally there are even small woods. Almost invariably the trees are evergreens—eastern red cedars and pines—though a unique type of small oak also seems to manage quite well.

In this sort of setting there is little to retain the water that falls so freely on the Southeast. Within a day of most rains, the granite is dry and lifeless-looking. For the plants, the mountain is essentially a desert. When water is plentiful, however, the mountain is a thing of beauty. Small streams lace the slopes with clear, pulsing rivulets and fill still pools with pure rainwater. Wet streaks slick the slopes, and if the rainfall has been heavy, two or three streams plunge noisily down waterworn grooves in the rock. Paved by granite and banked by mosses, the water carries no sediment. Momentarily it is water as timeless and pure as the sky from which it came.

An unceasing equilibrium between encroaching vegetation and erosion maintains these exposures at approximately the same size through the millennia. For at least two hundred and fifty million years the granite has been exposed: time far beyond the appearance of birds and mammals, the ice ages, and the advent of man. Time enough to evolve a botany perfectly adapted to its environment.

Plant life on the granite mountains, though within sight of the Blue Ridge, is quite different in appearance and origin from that of the highlands. In tracing the evolution of the botany in the two regions, scientists have concluded that both the southern highland and granite exposure plant groupings are extremely ancient. Beyond that, it has been ascertained that the highland flora is a descendant of a great forest type that is today present elsewhere only in Southeast Asia. Recent discoveries in geology, first proposed by the German meteorologist Alfred Wegener in 1912, have shown that the earth's landmass was once a single great continent. During some period of greater continental continuity, a botany developed that must have been contiguous. Later, long after the separation of the continents, the ice ages reduced the holdings of the great broadleaf forest to relatively small areas in the American Southeast and in Southeast Asia. From there it again spread until, at the time of the white man's coming to America, it covered much of what is now the eastern United States.

The plant life of the granite, on the other hand, came later and originated not from the Appalachian highlands but from the southwestern United States and the Mexican highlands. Only on a few dry, rocky mountains and outcrops could these desert plants survive in the Southeast. And because the surrounding plateaus and mountains were already occupied by vigorous forest, the desert plants were outcompeted in any attempts they might have made to move off the granite. The result, then, is a sixty-million-year-old botanical enclave, perfectly adapted to its surroundings, separated by half a continent from its nearest relatives, and found only on about eight thousand acres of granite.

So stable is the relationship between these plants and the granite that there is almost no tendency for the rock to be covered by vegetation. Yet this is not to say that the most persistent of plants don't work here as vigorously as they might on any rock. The granite is a great pioneering place for tenacious plants such as mosses and lichens. On the otherwise bare slopes of Stone Mountain are literally acres of mosses, mainly of the genus *Grimmia*. Gray until moisture vitalizes them, they then carpet the granite with a soft emerald-green mat. When small streams of sparkling water burst over them, they are an idyllic counterpoint to the rock upon which they live. *Cladonia* lichens, almost as tenacious as mosses, find footholds where even the slightest moisture can sustain them.

Botanists have discovered about two hundred species of plants which are closely associated with the granite exposures. Of the total, twelve are rare elsewhere and some seventeen grow nowhere else. Two of these are especially noticeable to the layman. For one of them, life begins in late February when the sun warms shallow depressions in the rock. In these sometimes wet but usually dusty depressions are the seeds of a tiny blood-red plant. *Diamorpha cymosa*, the species is called; there is no common name for this uncommon embellishment of nature. By early March almost every shallow depression is splashed with pools of crimson

Diamorpha. As the plants progress into flowering, miniature white blossoms appear over the inch-high stalks. By late April the plants have gone to seed and quietly disappeared, just as they have done for millions of years.

While photographing the plants one day, I paused to watch a young couple as they crossed a small area of granite set aside as a botanical preserve. Trailing them as they chatted and walked was a boy perhaps six years old. Seeing me crouched next to a crimson swash of the harmless plants, the boy knelt to touch them. "Stop. Get away. They're poison!" the mother shrieked. The boy jumped back, startled, and edged away. Not long after the three had disappeared toward their car, a trail biker came snarling over the granite. Glancing only briefly at the most extensive colonies of the tiny plant, he churned directly through them, sending drops of blood-red stalks in every direction.

For my own part, I have tried to develop a reverence for life. In this, I base my philosophy upon the idea that man cannot survive in his present condition without such an attitude. Our power to destroy is too great. The mother whose suspicion of nature had struck fear into her son undoubtedly would see little to commend my philosophy. By her actions, she perhaps has created another trail biker, and, like the present-day trail biker, has done her small part to keep many from whatever peace they can have with the earth.

Succeeding *Diamorpha* through the summer are other endemic plants, among them a species of St. John's wort (*Hypericum splendens*) that grows only on a few acres high on the west slope of Stone Mountain. By late June, when the shrubs produce their countless butter-yellow blossoms, the slopes are hot and inhospitable. Only the swarms of bees which seem to delight in these flowers seem to pay them much heed.

There comes a week in early September, however, when the attention of even the most casual visitors is captured. Within a few days of September tenth, the larger granite exposures are mantled with *Viguiera porteri*, a yellow daisylike composite that is found nowhere else. When the flower was discovered in 1846 by clergyman-botanist Dr. Thomas Porter, its genus was unknown. As it later turned out, *Viguiera* is a flower of the deserts. Though some species in the genus grow eastward as far as New Mexico and west Texas, the flower is at its best in the Old Southwest and Mexico. Only on the granite where the soil is thin and runoff is quick are conditions right for it in the Southeast. Profuse to the point of profligacy, the blossoms glow in the warm evening light of late summer. Set against the blue sky on a clear day or rippling in the first cool breezes of September, they form one of the world's great wildflower displays.

The moments in a person's life that seem touched by a genuine awe for the sheer munificence of nature are few, but when I count mine, a clear September day on the granite, with *Viguiera* in bloom everywhere, a fresh breeze blowing, and water seeping and splashing down the slopes, is remembered with the best of them. I walked that day, stopping often, feeling the coolness of morning, watching the bees work their golden world, smelling the freshness of the damp grasses, and compulsively touching great swaths of vibrant green moss. After wandering all morning, I rested and then returned as the mellowness of the late summer evening set in. In those hours, the physical presence of the land had been transmuted into the metaphysical by the catalyst of the person and the moment of being. The importance of such hours cannot be overestimated; they are so profound that their memory is intense to the end of life. When the day was over, it came to symbolize purity as it could be and had been for countless millennia in this place.

The wonder of the mountain, though, lies not just in its physical form or botanical uniqueness. Rather, it is that so few have truly discovered it. Perhaps in our cultural preoccupation with size, that equally important measure of a mountain's dimension—its extension into time—is explored by too few. Time, the ingredient bequeathed so bountifully upon nature and so parsimoniously to individual men, is here capable of transforming small importances into great events. The greening of the mosses, the erosive power of rain dropped from endless storms, brief encounters between predator and prey—these are the tickings of the aeons here. They have created on these granite mountains an ecological quintessence.

Ten years I roamed the slopes of those granite ancestors to the Appalachians. Nothing changed but me. With the passing years, experiences came to form the grand impression that I now retain of them. That impression is a matter of experiences more cumulative than immediate. Only very infrequently did events reach the intensity that builds strong recollections. The death pact in which I played a part was one of them.

Preoccupied with photography, I was standing motionless in a grove of stunted pines. As I studied my surroundings, a cottontail rabbit, its fear of me sublimated by a greater terror, approached to crouch at my side. Startled, I looked in the direction from which it had come. Lithe death was following it, darting

13

from rock to rock, searching it out with twitching nose and bright eyes. Brown, slender, and possessed by its mission, the predator—a weasel—failed to see me. Closer it came, close, too close, its intensity suddenly making me no longer a bystander. I moved. The pact was broken, and the two animals disappeared in opposite directions.

In almost the same place a few months later, I unexpectedly came face to face with a fox. Again, it was I who was motionless. The animal, rusty red with a white-tipped tail, trotted to within a few paces, stopped, and looked intently at me. I remained still. Ears forward, nose testing the air, he watched me uneasily. We stood that way until finally the situation became unbearable. As silently as he had come, he disappeared. At the very doorstep of Atlanta, the mountain is much as it always has been.

Moments have passed, too, when I understood that the mountain itself can be a predator. In the past century two dozen people have died on it, principally by falling a vertical five hundred feet from its north face. Dome-shaped, the mountain has few flat clifftops where one can walk to the edge for a view. The rock instead gets steeper by degrees. The urge is to descend a little farther in the hope of seeing over the edge. When finally the moment of reckoning comes, it may be too late to climb back. The way back up is less visible from below, a feeling of panic sets in, and reason is lost to the urge to climb at any cost. Security is staying put and waiting for rescue, but the mind rebels, the last fingerhold is lost, and the final slide becomes a free fall to death far below. So treacherous is the granite that a legend has grown up around the exploits of Elias Nour, a local resident who rescued dozens of people and innumerable pets from the mountain before 1950.

Perhaps the closest the mountain ever came to claiming me was in January 1970. During the night rain had soaked the Piedmont, and by morning temperatures were hovering just above freezing. Stone Mountain was closed in by clouds halfway to the top, but I climbed anyway. Perhaps two-thirds of the way up, I entered a world of ice-coated rock and rime-covered trees. In the fog the effect was pure fantasy. My rubber-soled boots, though safe on rock, did little good on the ice. Nevertheless, I continued to climb, chocking each step against gravel that had been laid down as part of the construction project for the summit building. As I neared the last steep slope, the sky began to clear. The upper slopes became a miniature world of alpine splendor that is seldom seen so far south.

Grabbing a thick, rusty cable that was secured from above, I began to haul myself beyond the gravel onto smooth rock and up the steep slope. The rock leveled not far above, but the going was slow. I was on pure ice, often on my knees, and the cable itself was sometimes icy. Backing down was out of the question. There was nothing left but to hold on and pull myself up. Though I climbed that way for perhaps only ten minutes, I was bruised and shaky when I could finally move away from the cable on almost level ice. For an hour I stayed just below the summit, first photographing the rime, clouds, and ice and then waiting for the sun to soften the frozen surface. But the way down was, if anything, worse. Almost back to the gravel again, I let go of the cable, stood up, and with one slight move fell flat. Nearly a week passed before the soreness wore off.

In general, the granite mountains were good to me. Eventually I moved away, perhaps never to see them again. But without them, my genesis as a naturalist and photographer would not have been possible. On them, I learned their beauty—and learned that people did not share my feeling. The granite had always been there, they'd all seen it, but almost none of them had any relationship with it. We think in patterns carved out and constrained by our culture; like our physical wanderings, our mental exploration of the world follows paths of direction set by others. When others neglect to point them out, beauty and knowledge are too often unseen.

For myself, the realization that living, dying, and again living are absolutely predictable and that they occur so inevitably was eventually felt as well as made known to me in the well-ordered universe on this granite-founded world. It is an important experience, this realization of the power of life given this planet. It provides perspective and hope.

Color Plates 1–23

1–5 Stone Mountain, Georgia: (1) Winter haze on the granite slopes; (2) a footworn summit trail; (3) green ribbons of mountain laurel at the base; (4) the glow of sunset on a red cedar; (5) and exfoliated granite.

6 Carpet of moss on the summit of Mount Panola, Georgia.

7 Beech forest at the foot of Stone Mountain.

8–10 *Diamorpha cymosa* on Stone Mountain.

11 *Viguiera porteri* in mid-September.

12 Encased in ice, a sparse Stone Mountain forest sparkles in the January sun.

13 Aftermath of an ice storm, Stone Mountain.

14 Roaring Fork Creek in Great Smoky Mountains National Park on the Tennessee–North Carolina border.

15 Springtime in a Georgia town.

16 A bald on Whitetop Mountain, Virginia, russet from the frosts and freezing of early October.

17 Dogwood, a cabin, and a springhouse in north Georgia.

18–22 Weathered wood, rusted iron, and the brittle leather of once-supple harnesses lie derelict on old farms.

23 Signs and posters in an abandoned store in Suches, Georgia.

16

3

2

4

5

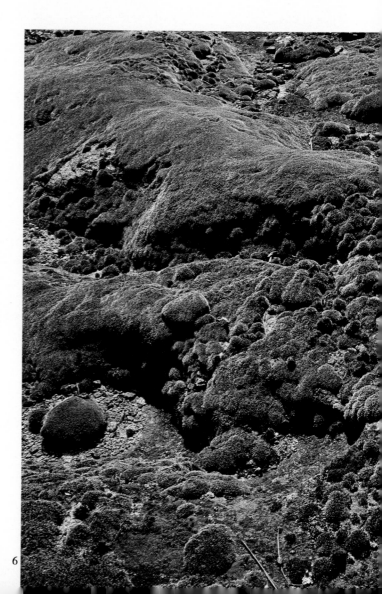

6

8

9

10

12

15

16

17

18

19

20

21

23

Broken Fields and Broken Horizons: The Southern Blue Ridge

Go anywhere in these mountains and you'll see them: the old fields and the mountains beyond. The plow and the ax bit deeply into this land and its forests, leaving scars that are well along toward being covered with new growth. Where once there were fields, orchards, and farms, pioneer plants such as broom sedge, kudzu, pines, yellow poplars, and oaks are now dressing the wounds. From the wilderness enthusiast's viewpoint, the old farmlands and young forests may not be attractive, but they are a ubiquitous part of the Blue Ridge, and as such join with the remaining untouched forests to weave the fabric of these mountains today. And in their own right, the broken fields possess a certain beauty and promise.

Of all the pioneer plants, broom sedge is probably the most widespread on old fields. In the warmer months its tender tallgrass stalks blend with other plant growth, but in winter it distinctively fringes the fields in colors that range from a dull brown on dry days to a rich rusty orange in wet weather. Broom sedge is one of those field grasses that look as though an artist had invented them for effect. The color is melancholy and in keeping with winter on the old farms. Standing in a field of broom sedge on a windy and moonlit winter night, one can hear the whispering stalks and sense surges of movement created by the wind. The tallgrass is perhaps responding not just to wind but to the toil of the tired and troubled men who kept at the land far too long.

Kudzu, on the other hand, has little to recommend it. An Oriental vine, it was introduced to combat erosion, but it has multiplied so much that in places its leafy tendrils cover trees and otherwise barren ground with undulating seas of green leaves. "Keeping down the kudzu" has become an accepted part of farming on the warmer slopes of the Blue Ridge. If nothing else, the strangulating seas of vines have been good cause for humor and sarcasm, and perhaps some service has even been done in containing the soil.

Kudzu is an alternative to a process in which crabgrass and horseweed may begin covering old fields and are then replaced by asters and broom sedge. With the plants live characteristic animals and insects. The least shrew, old-field mouse, and harvest mouse—the latter two often heard but seldom seen in my experience—appear almost as soon as weeds take over bare fields. In the second year of old-field succession, bobwhites and eastern meadowlarks are common, and by the third year cottontail rabbits appear.

Where the forest has begun to take over from the fields, the aspect becomes less pleasing. The piny woods are sterile places not given to any great diversity in plant growth. Thick tangles of dead limbs and dry, crackly duff impart a lifeless look to these forests. Only lichens seem to succeed on the forest floor. Put in perspective, however, the piny woods have their attributes. The soil from which they grow is impoverished, and without them it would grow little at all.

On the Blue Ridge, pines usually appear on old fields after about six years. Principally these are loblolly and shortleaf pines, except farther north or at higher elevations, where Virginia pines take over. As the pines grow, the animals and insects that had once lived in the old fields give way to forest species. When the pines are from twenty to twenty-five years old, the first broadleaf trees—usually sweet gum or yellow poplars—begin to compete with the pines. In thirty or forty years oaks and hickories, the usual climax species, are present. Even in the temperate climate of the Blue Ridge, the process of plant succession is a long one.

In many of the mountain valleys plant growth has proceeded enough so that a respectable forest covers unused lands. The bottomlands near Oconaluftee in Great Smoky Mountains National Park are a familiar example, and so are the ridge forests along many miles of the Blue Ridge Parkway and Skyline Drive. At Oconaluftee the river "bottoms" were mostly in pasture or cropland fifty years ago. Today the yellow poplars are fifty or sixty feet tall and are beginning to look as if they'd been there forever. With the exception of a certain tidiness typical of National Park Service lands, the scene is much like that of many Blue Ridge Mountain valleys. Farms and mills like those at Oconaluftee could be seen elsewhere, but here they are restored and kept in operation.

Agricultural areas in the Blue Ridge today have few ideal-looking farms. Weatherbeaten, a little ragged with age, they look back to better years. Those that survive usually do so because their land is better for farming than those of earlier competitors. Driving the back roads, one sees houses in all stages of repair and disrepair. Some few still serve as farmhouses; most are homes for people who have jobs elsewhere or who have retired themselves along with their farms. The barns, even in their best days, never compared with their large counterparts in the northern states. Somewhere in size between sheds and barns, they are as characteristic of the South as the Pennsylvania Dutch barns are of eastern Pennsylvania. Good enough to put a mule or plowhorse and a few tools in, they nevertheless served their purpose well. "MAIL POUCH" or "SEE ROCK CITY," the barn roofs sometimes proclaim, but more often their flat tin sheathing is patterned with bright orange rust.

I like this country. It is uncrowded, unnoticed, and despite its trailers and junkyards, it speaks strongly about its past. The country churches are kept up, the people have taken the trouble to plant beds of flowering thrift and yellow daffodils, and there is space enough between neighbors so that a person needn't be bothered by noise. Because the old farmlands are so prevalent, I have spent many hours exploring them by car and on foot. Emergent from all this is a personal impression of people who are dissimilar in the sense of being individuals, but who are very much the heirs of a shared heritage.

During my explorations I inevitably got into trouble. Privacy is not to be lightly contended with, especially when the use of a camera is involved. One farmer, in response to my asking, let me photograph the interior of his barn on two occasions, once while he watched and again while he went about his business. The third time I came back, no one was at home. I finished my photography anyway and was just about to leave when he returned.

"You been in the barn?" He bristled. I admitted it.

"You ain't never comin' back here agin." He leveled the words at me as if they were blasts from a shotgun. He was right. I never went back.

Unusual settings or activities always cause me to reach for my camera. Some are supremely easy to photograph; others are risky. Farmers using horses or mules for plowing have been perhaps the most difficult subjects for me. They're busy and don't want to be bothered, or, likely as not, the animal shies at the sight of someone crouched with a camera. But at least I ask. For the most part, people try to be accommodating.

"You go ahead," a weatherbeaten old man with an equally worn mule replied cryptically as I approached and indicated I'd like a picture. Satisfied, I began setting up the camera. He turned and began working another furrow, gee-hawing at the mule in a way that only a man who knows his animal can talk. Back at my end of the cornpatch again, he stopped and looked at me squarely.

"I thought I told you to go ahead," he said, the impatience in his voice turning to anger. "Now go ahead!" The idea that he meant for me to leave got through to me immediately. I picked up the camera and left, not even bothering to turn around when I heard his muletalk and the clank of the plow begin again.

I have met many people with whom I fared better, however, much as I did when I was searching the back roads of the Blue Ridge in north Georgia one late summer morning. Quite unexpectedly I chanced upon a covered bridge and below it saw a small creek sweeping broadly over worn rocks. The place was overgrown, silent, and seemingly forgotten by time and the outside world. Dimly, through a thick screen of second-growth forest, I perceived something else too: a ghost of a building, an abandoned mill.

Nothing better represents the culture of the Blue Ridge people than their water mills. Like all of the Appalachians, the Blue Ridge was ideal country for water power. Abundant rainfall, numerous streams, and plenty of wood and stone with which to construct the mills, all combined to create a situation in which mills were located at nearly all shoals and rapids. By the 1890s water power was in many places grinding grain and even powering machines for the industrial New South.

To the Blue Ridge farmer, however, the only mill was the grist mill. It spoke his thoughts about the ways in which native materials should be combined, and it answered his need for cornmeal, flour, and conversation. Through the years from the mid-1700s until the 1940s, millwrights designed from wood, stone, and iron an ever more ingenious technology. Crude tub mills, quaint water-wheel mills, and highly efficient turbine mills succeeded one another through the years in serving southern farmers. By World War II, however, most of them had ceased functioning as commercial operations.

The mill I was approaching turned out to be turbine powered. A three-story frame building, it stood high above the creek on a steep bank. Broken sections of corrugated metal pipe, half hidden by honeysuckle, marked the route by which water had reached the mill's penstock, a once-towering wooden and water-filled shaft. The weight of the water escaping from beneath the penstock had powered the mill's twin turbines, which then sent power to the milling machinery through a system of belts and wheels. Built in 1902 and operated until 1942, the mill contained both traditional millstones for grinding corn and a complete flour mill for making high-quality wheat flour. When the milling machines were installed by the Indianapolis firm of Nordyke and Marmon, they represented state-of-the-art technology. In the context of its time that technology was in no way inferior to today's technology.

In the sunshine of this day the rusted iron machinery lay scattered in a deep pit where the penstock had stood. The building itself was a testimony to times past—and a photographic imperative for me. I shoved through a thick tangle of mountain laurel, set my tripod on the stream bank, attached the camera, and pulled the focusing cloth over my head. When I pulled away the cloth, a middle-aged man in bib overalls was right beside me.

"What you *doin'* here?" he demanded.

Lean, tanned, suspicious, and agitated, he was ready to speak for the place. "You from the power company?" He looked at the camera. "I thought you was surveyin'."

It wasn't the first or last time I'd encountered that question. The Blue Ridge has been exploited by everything from lumber companies to second home developers, and the hatred for surveyors runs deep. I explained myself, though not to his complete satisfaction. He couldn't quite understand why I wanted to photograph an old mill, yet the idea that I wasn't a surveyor was a big relief. Both of us relaxed some. The property wasn't his legally, he admitted, but he'd grown up nearby and that was enough. We talked about the mill for a few minutes, and, somewhat more at ease, he left.

The people who live in these hills and hollows have long addressed themselves to such problems as land acquisition and "development." Proud of what they have accomplished, and threatened by its destruction, they react with predictable enmity toward those who continue to brush them aside. "Bring us your civilization, but leave us our culture," one of them once told an outsider. New civilizations and old cultures, unfortunately, do not abide peaceably. Places where time seems to have stopped are seldom seen today, and even less often does one find places that seem to speak for all the others that were once like them.

But perhaps of all such places, it is country stores that remain the most obvious. The old stores, with

37

gas pumps in front, general merchandise stacked ceiling-high on behind-the-counter shelves, old stoves in the back, and faded chewing tobacco ads, are still around.

Several old gaffers sat talking on benches arranged along the front of a store I walked into one day. They were watching me as I came, and I knew it, but I wanted to see the store as much as I had wanted to see the mill. Walking through the open front door, I beheld a scene of general but obviously functional clutter. Through the years the store's arrangement had probably evolved in a trial-and-error manner. It was hot that day and even more so in the store. Hot enough to keep a dog panting—which is what a large black-and-white mongrel was doing as he sat just inside the door, drooling copiously into a wooden bin of large, pale onions. The animal's attention was riveted on a cookie a heavyset man at the counter was eating. Neither dog nor human paid me much attention as I looked the store over, next noticing a round of cheese that was centered on an ancient iron cheese slicer. Equally old and even more battered, a brown cash register occupied the end of the well-worn counter. While the man with the dog talked to the proprietor, I explored the store. A few flies buzzed unhurriedly from shelf to can, but in general there was little they could contaminate.

Even in the old stores, the merchandise is new, and this one was no exception. Only the arrangement and selection of the items betrayed the store's function in the area. Shoes, enamel pots and pans, iron skillets, axes, insect repellent, and detergent were all shelved in no apparent order. Most of what a person might need on short notice was included. On the wall a Chesterfield cigarette sign from the 1940s completed the decor. This was the sort of place where things just accumulate until they disintegrate from age. Seeing nothing that I needed and little that I could photograph, I turned without any further hesitation and left. Months later I walked into a similar store, this one run by a proud elderly couple. Without my asking, they moved together behind the counter to be photographed. The result was a picture that transcends time and place to speak for all small proprietary stores.

If the stores seem to betray anything about the southern mountain people, it is their sense of community. People know their neighbors in these hills and are quite willing to judge them. It is a society in which the store, the coon hunt, the gas station, and the telephone serve as mediums for the exchange of endless opinionating. Everybody either knows what is going on or soon finds out about it. Newcomers are always carefully distinguished from old families and are assimilated very slowly. But then, every culture has ways of preserving itself, and these people are only sharing the traits of country people everywhere.

No one spoke to me in the store. There was no need—the store spoke for the people. Yet there are times when what has been said is the essence of an experience. Miles distant from the store is an old farmhouse. Simple and sturdy in design, it rests beneath a large oak tree. Splashing color along its weathered board siding, a country-style garden of roses and sweet Williams outcompetes whatever weeds might dare to invade it. Like the mill and store, it is an enclave in time.

Intent on asking permission to photograph the house, I turned the crank bell at the front door. Voices from within confirmed that people were home, yet no one answered. Fighting the feeling that I shouldn't wander so far onto the premises unannounced, I walked around the house past the well and to the back door. It was open, and through the screen I saw an old couple seated at the kitchen table.

"Hello," I ventured. "Would you mind if I took some pictures of your house?"

The old man looked at the woman. He saw me but couldn't hear. "Come in," she answered, brushing aside the question. "Would you like some lunch?"

I entered the kitchen, surprised at her acceptance of a stranger at the door. "No," I answered. "It's just that I like to take pictures of old houses and barns. I don't want to bother you." But I saw that I was wrong in not accepting. Stranger or not, I was in her kitchen, there was food on the table, and it would be an insult to her hospitality to refuse the offer. "If you have enough, I could use some lunch," I said.

The food was southern, delicious, and a prime example of the expertise that comes from years of traditional cooking. Potato pie, served hot from a flat pan, was the main dish. Sweetened and browned to perfection, it was smooth and properly served with tea (iced tea in the North; just "tea" here). Feeling awkward, but greedy for more, I protested only slightly when she offered to refill my plate. There was corn, too—and okra, finely seasoned and fried. I took helpings of both.

We talked a little. Where was I from, they wanted to know. That question must always be answered when you are talking to people in the South. They knew people in my town with names I could at least recall. That helped. When the tea was finished, they asked if I liked old pictures. Yes, I answered, and was shown to the dining room, where loose photographs by the dozens were pulled from a drawer in the sideboard.

In the photographs was a grand pageant of southern history—the Scotch-Irish who had settled these hills, the inevitable Civil War soldiers in new uniforms, and more recent generations of prosperous-looking merchants and farmers. Ambrotypes, tintypes, sepia-toned prints, portraits by commercial studios, and a modern color snapshot or two were scattered across the table as if someone had flung a handful of years there.

"Take care of these pictures," I urged loudly to the old man. "People collect pictures like these now. They're valuable."

"We don't have any use for them," his wife replied, obviously unimpressed. Leaving it at that, they showed me the rest of the house. The rooms, largely unused, were filled with furniture from the 1890s and early 1900s. For a collector, the place would have been a paradise.

As we again entered the dining room, they talked of giving the photographs to their relatives. As far as they were concerned, the collection contained too many pictures of forgotten forebears. "If they don't want them, you can have them," the old man suddenly said. I expressed an interest but knew they'd tell their family that a stranger would take the photos. New value would then be attached to them. I have not been back, but I have no doubt that the pictures now repose in the drawer of some younger relative.

When I left that house, the afternoon sun shown warmly on a countryside filled with the expectation of autumn. Weeks passed before I was able to explore again, but when I did, autumn was itself a memory. January had come, and on that day the wind blew bitterly through the woods and across the empty fields. With each fresh gust, drafts of icy air surged past loose windowpanes and into the empty classrooms of an abandoned school. I was alone, and for as much time as I wished to give it, the building was mine.

I had been driving along back roads months earlier when I first saw the school, a rambling old building set just down from several houses of 1910 vintage. I tried the door that day, found it padlocked, and later inquired about the school of a country physician I knew. Phone calls were made, the word went out that I could be trusted, and two weeks later an old man who lived near the school provided me with a key. If anyone had been in the building since the day it closed its doors in May 1933, there was no sign of it.

Moving silently, listening to every creak and shudder the wind was drawing from the place, I searched. A portrait of George Washington, exactly like those dimly remembered from my elementary-school days, hung prominently on a classroom wall. A potbellied stove, solid as the day its last embers had grown cold, stood front-and-center. School desks, the wood-and-iron sort with folding seats and inkwells in the tops, marched in rows across the room or were stacked haphazardly in the back. "20th Century. Sears, Roebuck & Co. Chicago," they proclaimed in ornate letters. On the blackboard was an admonition, written by hands now grown old, cheering on the Central School. A page of poetry torn from a reader lay across a seat. "Dead on the Cuban Shore," the first selection was entitled. Below it "Our Heroes" spoke stridently of those Spanish-American War heroes Dewey and Sampson and Schley. Dust had settled on everything, but the humanity of the place was still evident. Initials carved in the desks and seats worn smooth by countless skirts and britches spoke of the energetic children who had spent hours there. For as long as the cold would let me, I moved about the room, trying to imprint what I had seen onto film and mind.

Upstairs, where the wind showed its eagerness even more, a silent, dusty auditorium waited in the gloom. A wooden pump organ, its works beyond repair, stood next to a window. A moment in time— perhaps May 25, 1933, at three o'clock—hung suspended. The wind shook the building perceptibly.

The Great Depression was a time for change not only in the Blue Ridge but everywhere. Disaster, in forms both economic and natural, stalked the land. In these mountains the general pattern was the same; only the specifics were different. By the 1930s the hills had essentially been lumbered out, overfarmed, and scarred by erosion. It was time for a change.

People moved away, schools like the Central School closed, and the government moved in. These were the years of the political Great Divide in America. Before them government had been small and remote; after them it became a dominant force in American life. In the Blue Ridge, national forests and parks were established, roads were built across the mountains and into the hollows, and a people who had grown poor working with the land entered the mainstream of American economic life. With the coming of World War II, the process was accelerated. Though the older generation tended to stay in the hills and hollows of their homeland, the cultural chain that is forged by the melding of generations was broken.

The old are mostly alone now; the world they knew is far enough removed by technology and social change from that of today that they see few of us accepting their way of life, with its sense of place and unquestioned values. The bitterness I have so often heard in their voices is not just a mark of age—it is the sound of despair. Like most of us past childhood, they cannot return to the places of their youth. And, uniquely among generations, they do not see many of their life patterns, habits, and values serving as guiding principles in modern society. Memories must suffice, though the urge to know again those places of youth is perhaps strongest as one nears the close of life. "I am writing to you about this place. . . ." a letter I received recently began.

> Now I was up there about 3 years ago. Nothing standing but old store building and a half of a old white brick wall. I understand it has gone through of lots of land owner the last one I knew of . . . that was 50 years ago. I . . . hope some where and some how. you can find out something. it would make me so happy and to know where my father was raised. (that was 1875)
>
> With best of luck and God Bless you.
Lessie Brown Tanner

She wanted to know--to return in her way once again—but the town is gone; only the mountains remain. Beyond letting her know that I could try, there was little I could do for her.

Perhaps the letter was answered as best it could have been by a friend who had known her once in that place, in their youth. Both of them knew that the town—the sense of community there, its impact on those who lived in it—is lost to youth in the metropolitan rootlessness of modern America. To her and all those who share the small-town heritage, he could at least say that the value of their town and of the others like them far surpasses brick and mortar.

All my family was a way for years. I returned to find out the places although dead, had left a rich and indelisble inheratage, kind and thoughtful descendants. They in that, if nothing else, will keep the embers burning until some wind of good fortune enclindles the flame anew, I join you in the spirit of best wishes for the old communities—

Respt yours truly
John McKeon

But the legacy of the mountain people is not completely lost. Of late there has been widespread interest in researching, restoring, and remembering the best the mountain culture had to offer. In publications like the *Foxfire* books initiated at the Rabun Gap–Nacoochee School in north Georgia and the *Goldenseal* magazine of West Virginia's state Arts and Humanities Council, the old ways are treated with reverence. Time-honored philosophies and practices are orally recorded and then transcribed into print. And the audience is wide. People want to know how quilts were made, hogs were slaughtered, medicines were blended, log cabins were built, music was played, and any of hundreds of other things accomplished. The publications tell them.

At arts and crafts fairs both young and old work side by side to perpetuate mountain cultural specialties. At a craft fair I visited recently with my family, my wife talked with an elderly couple who were making baskets. "They were making baskets from oak just as they'd been taught from childhood," she told me. "The husband was earning five dollars a day at his job, but when he found that he could earn six dollars by making baskets, he quit and hasn't done anything but make baskets since. Then Colonial Williamsburg saw some of their baskets and realized that they were making them in authentic eighteenth-century style. Williamsburg has been placing orders regularly, and at the craft fairs the bigger baskets are bringing thirty-five dollars each. And still they have more orders than they can fill."

That interest in some measure reflects the tendency of Americans to collect things. But it is more than that alone. It is a recognition of the Appalachian folk culture as an authentic art source. Pottery, painting, quilting, furniture making, leather working, porcelain painting, and numerous other arts and crafts all attract enthusiastic audiences. The people of the Blue Ridge have been able after all to pass on something of what they have been and done.

When the first generations of these people settled in the Blue Ridge, theirs was a world incredibly green and lush. Deep valleys, most of them narrow with rushing streams, but some broad and blessed by a thick covering of soil, contrasted sharply with the high surrounding mountains. When the whites arrived, many of the valleys contained great stands of ancient trees. Botanists look upon the remnants of this forest with wonder, noting the profusion of plant species which the valleys harbored. This was the heart of the Appalachian forest, with places like the well-watered mountain "coves" (enclosed valleys) where more kinds of deciduous trees grow than are native to all of western Europe.

Inventories of the botany have revealed 130 species of trees, 1400 species of flowering herbs, 350 species of mosses and related plants, and 2000 species of fungi. Even today there are enough remnants of this forest to show a person just what the original Appalachian forest was really like. Undisturbed mountain coves are the best places to see this forest. In the coves exists a stage of forest life in which the species of plants and animals remain constant in proportion and kind over the centuries. Barring some natural or human-inspired catastrophe, the giant trees grow old, die, and rot, only to be replaced by others of their kind. This is a forest in which each living thing plays a role that closely affects every other component of the forest. Over the millennia the forest system has grown so interrelated that it is like a single giant organism. Small wounds can be repaired, but the destruction of the large members of the forest would spell the end for all its lesser components. Only through the long process of plant succession could the forest then recreate itself.

Where remnants of the great Appalachian cove forest remain, life is at a metabolic minimum. Great hemlocks and yellow poplars, straight and tall, shut out the sunlight with their crowns. Only where the giants have fallen do large numbers of young trees grow vigorously in patches of light. There is a silence in these great valley forests broken only by birds high in the trees or the sound of creeks running over mossy boulders. The Joyce Kilmer Memorial Forest in the Snowbird Range of North Carolina is an unsurpassed example, as are the cove forests of the Great Smoky Mountains National Park and the Linville Gorge Wilderness Area.

Vast though it was, by the late 1920s the forest was mostly a thing of the past. Industry and agriculture took some of it, and lumbermen eliminated much of the rest. Logging was easily the most destructive of the abuses man wrought in the Blue Ridge. Lumbermen dragged trees down slopes to railroads, ripping the soil open as they went. The shade was gone, the soil was destroyed, and erosion set in. Creeks and rivers overflowed their banks and became filled with sediment. When the large-scale logging was over, the great Appalachian forest had been opened by man.

In its diversity and composition, the forest of cove and valley remains unique, yet it is not the only Blue Ridge forest. Between three thousand and five thousand feet along the Blue Ridge the trees are mainly those species which are more common to the northern states. This is the northern hardwoods forest. A mixture of sugar maples, beeches, buckeyes, and other northern species blends with more southern species to give this forest the colors of autumn reminiscent of New England. The gently rolling farm country of southwestern Virginia and northwestern North Carolina near Mount Rogers National Recreation Area and Grayson Highlands State Park, Virginia, are excellent places to see this forest and its autumn color. Perhaps one of the more unusual aspects of this northern hardwoods forest occurs along some of the high ramparts of the Blue Ridge where northern red oaks occur in pure stands at elevations of four thousand to five thousand feet. When this happens, as it does at Apple Orchard Mountain, Virginia, and Craggy Gardens in North Carolina, the slopes are often covered with dwarf forests known as "orchards."

High on the ridges, where even the northern hardwoods find the climate too taxing, grows a forest of spruce and fir with a mood, presence, and composition that belong to it alone. In the thickness of this green, mossy setting, sounds are muffled by the growth, and once again little can be heard but the constant calls of birds or the wind washing through the firs. The sense of smell is awakened by pervasive fragrances, especially those of the firs. Open views are the exception, but the high country does well without them. Along the trails the forest floor is carpeted with moss and patterned by ferns. Northern wildflowers, such as wood sorrel and dwarf dogwood (bunchberry), brighten green forest pathways. Birds of the northern forest—juncos, winter wrens, black-throated blue warblers, and veeries—make these peaks home. Beginning on the south at Tanasee Bald along the Blue Ridge Parkway near Brevard, North Carolina, the spruce-fir forest skips across the valleys to touch the highest peaks in the East. Northward, it is encountered at lower elevations, and in Shenandoah National Park traces of it are seen on Stony Man and Hawksbill mountains at elevations close to four thousand feet. Westward beyond the Blue Ridge the spruce-fir forest dominates the Alleghenies at elevations of thirty-five hundred feet.

The sort of setting that suits these trees is both cold and wet. Temperatures decrease at a rate of about 2.23 degrees Fahrenheit per thousand feet; in the six-thousand-foot elevations of the high Blue Ridge, this produces a climate equal to one thousand miles northeast at sea level. Precipitation increases so dramatically that it may almost double on the peaks, reaching eighty inches per year or more in some locations. Fraser fir is the dominant tree above six thousand feet, and between five thousand and six thousand feet it shares the peaks with red spruce. Of the two trees, red spruce is much the larger, often reaching a hundred and fifty feet in height, five feet in diameter, and living to be three hundred years old. In contrast, firs are normally less than forty feet tall and are relatively short-lived because their susceptibility to wind damage severely limits their age. The elevational distribution of the two species has at least two explanations. Spruce can tolerate warmer temperatures than fir, but fir seeds can root and grow better through the moss of the higher elevation forest floor. Yet in the scattered high places where spruce does dominate, it tends to hold its ground against firs by growing taller and resisting windstorms better.

Very often the coniferous forests of the high Blue Ridge are referred to as Canadian Zone forests, the reference being to a system of describing mountain forests and associated wildlife developed by C. Hart Merriam of the U.S. Biological Survey in the 1890s. In the life-zone system elevational bands on mountains were compared to their sea-level counterparts farther north. The terms used were (from the south) Desert, Transition, Canadian, Hudsonian, and Arctic-Alpine. The system relied too heavily on comparative temperatures and was based on observations in Arizona, yet it was convenient and soon was widely utilized. Though it is used even today in popular literature, it is no longer considered adequate by biologists.

In some high gaps where spruce and fir should hold undisputed claim, almost pure stands of beech trees grow instead. The explanation seems to be that the spruce-fir forest was forced out during a time of warmer climate. Return of the conifers has been prevented because the solid carpet of beech leaves on the forest floor in these gaps is a barrier the conifer seeds cannot readily penetrate.

While northern forests are exceptional in the southern Appalachians, they are no more than variations in the great sea of trees that covers the peaks and valleys. Unique in the scheme of things here are the balds and grasslands. Balds are openings, usually small and above five thousand feet, that seem to be natural in origin. Scientists have pondered these areas for decades, catalogued their plants, divided them into grass and heath balds, but have been repeatedly thwarted in their attempts to explain them. The openings might possibly have been created by Indians, by elk and bison, climatic changes, or soil conditions— no one can yet say. Whatever their origin, they are welcome. The views from them are worthy, and the flowering rhododendron and laurel which grace them create spectacular natural gardens.

In contrast, the grasslands in North Carolina's Shining Rock Wilderness and Virginia's Mount Rogers National Recreation Area are easily explained. Loggers denuded these mountains, and fires then scorched away much of the soil. Today these areas are slices of Wyoming set in the South. Wind country, you might call the prairie crests, for here, a mile and more above sea level, the air flows constantly across the grass and the clouds wipe the land with their dampness. Ravens and an occasional golden eagle tumble and soar across the heavens, seemingly exuberant in their freedom to ride the wind. Watching a pair of ravens recently as they flew side by side in arcs and swoops and raised their voices to the heights, I could only conclude that their purposes were no more utilitarian than feeling the wind on their wings. Until we learn the language of birds, none of us can understand such actions. At best we can enjoy and admire them, perhaps imparting to the ravens emotions that we unknowingly share with them.

But if there is joy in the unknown, there must also be danger. Nature does not distinguish between

47

the two; she only presents the possibility of both. For myself, the possibility became a reality one warm afternoon on a grassy ridge in Virginia. Most of the afternoon a timber rattlesnake had been hunting through the tall grass. Moving steadily in response to warm June sunshine, it sought out rabbits, meadow voles—any prey of opportunity. For its kind the snake was rather large—approximately four and a half feet long. Thick-bodied and heavy, it was powerful, fast, and lethal to the largest prey it might encounter. Sensing the vibrations of my approaching footsteps, it hesitated.

The effects of a rattlesnake bite are, in the word of herpetologists, "horrendous." While the venom of a rattlesnake may not be as toxic as that of an Indian cobra, the rattlesnake is far better equipped to deliver it. Fangs an inch and a half long placed well forward in its jaws nearly always sink deeply into the victim. The venom, once delivered, works inexorably, turning tissue to jelly and causing agonizing pain. For a hundred-and-thirty-five-pound individual such as myself, death could come in a few hours.

The grass on all sides was thick and waist-high, but I had not been thinking of snakes. Moving at a medium stride through the field, I was concentrating on wildflowers at the instant of confrontation. Not three paces ahead, unseen, the snake buzzed loudly. The effect was electric. Never had I heard a rattlesnake or even seen one alive in the wild, but instantly—even instinctively—I planted both feet in place. Called up from some primordial source was the same sort of physical reaction that pulls the flesh from a hot object or shuts the eyes to bright light. Beyond doubt, I knew it was a rattlesnake.

Circling wide the spot where the buzzing continued, but still wanting to see the snake through the tall grass, I made approaches from several sides. When I finally saw the snake, it was drawing into a coil. The hair raised on my back and neck at the sight. The wide, wedge-shaped head was pointed directly at me, and the patterned brown-and-black body was nearly poised and ready to lunge. Fighting the urge to leave, I approached just beyond what I considered striking range to take some pictures. The grass was too tall and thick, though, and the photos show more grass than rattlesnake.

Only two species of venomous snakes inhabit the Blue Ridge—the timber rattler and the copperhead—yet fear of snakes runs deep among the people of these hills. Almost any pretext will be used to justify killing the most harmless of snakes. "They mate with copperheads," I have been told about blacksnakes. Or "They'll hoop up and roll along after you." No matter how tall the tale, it is told with conviction and fear. Before the day of the rattler, I laughed at those people. But the snake is still with me when I walk now. Even though I left that snake with neither of us the worse for wear, their fear is to a small degree my fear. Within hours of writing this, I was resting for a few minutes on a warm hillside, my eyes closed, my mind drifting. From the dead leaves not six inches from my right ear came a sound—not a four-footed or even a two-legged sound, but a smooth, gliding sound. Without a thought beyond that of "snake!" I shot straight up as if launched by a spring, and stood looking at the place where my head had been. For a minute I couldn't pick it out, so perfect was the camouflage. Then, suddenly, I saw it—a harmless garter snake about eighteen inches long. The responses the rattlesnake had confirmed were still with me.

Most often it is the weather that provokes caution. Beyond prediction sometimes, it can unexpectedly revert to the edge of the great Ice Age in winter—as it did one cold, dun-colored, and dormant day in western North Carolina. Nothing moved under endless gray sky, and there was no expectation of storm or clearing that afternoon. It was simply the sort of day when the trees stretch their skeletons against brown slopes and the ridges turn deep purple with distance. Perhaps the monotony of what I was seeing as I drove westward up the mountains deceived me. At any rate, I should have known the high country better and been prepared when I reached the divide at fifty-three hundred feet. Over the high slopes in front of me, along the walls of a broad valley below, and to the depths of its river-cut ravine, clouds had lain a great swath of frozen vapor through the brown forest. Clinging to every tree, cone, and needle, it covered each surface so completely that nothing of the substance beneath showed. Every bit of vegetation seemingly had been replaced by a pure white casting of itself.

Frozen cloud vapor, correctly known as rime but usually called hoarfrost by the people of the Blue Ridge, is a worldwide phenomenon of mountains. Unlike frost, it accumulates horizontally, with the thickest coatings on the windward sides of vegetation. Not a creature of cold, clear nights, but rather of the icy caress of cold, moist clouds, it touches every part of the Blue Ridge. Always it is the same, with delicacy far surpassing that of snow, and a fragility that causes it to melt or evaporate at the first suggestion of warm sunshine.

When I think of that afternoon on the divide, I feel again the utter surprise of that moment. Until I saw a lingering layer of stratus in the valley, I had been unaware of any recent low clouds. But the impact was perhaps greatest because the rime was thick and flawless where it existed, yet wholly absent outside the valley. The ridges beyond were untouched; against the rime they appeared to be jet black. As I stood watching in the bitter cold silence of that late afternoon, a streak of peach-colored sky spread across the horizon to the west, then slowly disappeared, taking with it the last of the day. As darkness fell, the cold and the stillness moved in just as they must have during the centuries when the glaciers lay just beyond the northern Blue Ridge.

In a sense, the mood and eloquence of mountains is the gift of clouds. A touch of rime, a wash of rain, the thickness of summit fog, and the promise of sunrise—all are cloud-given. And in mountains the presence of clouds may even be felt when the lowlands lie hot and hazy. On such a morning early in July, a hiking companion and I were well entrenched in sleeping bags high atop 6594-foot Mount Le Conte in the Great Smokies. With the first suggestion of dawn, we dressed and headed through a dark tunnel of firs toward Myrtle Point, a high, open shoulder of Mount Le Conte. In the forest nothing moved. There were no sounds except our own, and even these were muffled by the dense branches and mossy forest floor. We were a quarter of a mile down the trail and moving fast when we surprised a bear. Hissing like a pig, it edged into the woods. Cautiously, and then with speed again, we moved on.

Only then did we break into the clear. Light, clouds, wind, and the vast, mist-shrouded emptiness of the mountains caught us in one swift crescendo. But we were determined to see the sun rise, and this was not the place. Moving fast, we kept on toward Myrtle Point. When finally we broke out of the forest again, the dawn prelude was in progress. A layer of clouds swept silently by just above us; below were valleys without

50

number, and to the northeast was the first glow of the coming day. In the lowlands dewy fields lay limp under a still, cloudless sky. Here the world was an uneasy caldron of shifting clouds and uncertain winds deciding, before dawn, what should be done with the day.

While we watched, the valleys below, misty purple until dawn, glowed orange with the rising sun. In coloration, scope, and subject, the sunrise perfectly matched the work of nineteenth-century Romantic landscapist Albert Bierstadt. If I doubted the veracity of his work before then, I became convinced from that moment on. Then, just as the early light suffused into a yellow glow, the clouds lowered. The mountains were gone, a cold, damp wind sapped our resolve, and we left. Before we had reached camp, a soft rain was wetting the firs.

Color Plates 24–50

24 Tanner's Mill, Georgia. Early December.

25 Abandoned farm field.

26 Cabin in a clearing in Grayson County, Virginia.

27 Spring plowing.

28 Pastureland, Grayson County.

29 Farm pond, Jefferson County, West Virginia.

30 Cable Mill, Great Smoky Mountains National Park.

31–34 A worn chair, a display case left on a back porch, a faded album, and a Georgia plain-style house.

35, 36 Closed since 1933, a mountain school waits out its last years.

37 A country store in north Georgia and its proud proprietors.

38, 39 Rime on the heights of the Great Smoky Mountains and on Mount Yonah in Georgia.

40–42 Yellow slime mold, brown-scalloped bracket fungi, and oyster fungi create patterns and sculpture in the damp forests.

43 *Trillium grandiflorum* (snow trillium).

44 Hepatica and fern fiddleheads.

45 Yellow lady's-slipper.

46 *Trillium luteum.*

47 Bloodroot.

48 *Trillium erectum.*

49 Daisies.

50 Catawba rhododendron along the Blue Ridge Parkway at Craggy Gardens, North Carolina.

25

26

28

27

29

31

32

33

36

37

40

41

Wilderness Renewed:
The Northern Blue Ridge

When the winter wind moans through the empty forests of Shenandoah National Park, the sounds of the past ride with it. In the rustle of dry oak leaves, a thousand bygone hearth fires crackle to life. Rushes of wind through snowy hemlocks harmonize with forgotten tunes from long-silent fiddles and dulcimers. And the ice-rimmed brooks carry with them the sounds of mountain children's laughter and women's tears. If the sounds are an elegy, it is not meant to be so. The sadness is in the minds of men who mourn the passing of the old ways and youth. For those who listen to the present, there are new sounds: laughter, not tears, and camp stoves, not hearth fires. Since 1936 Shenandoah has been a place where people come only to enjoy the mountain world of the Blue Ridge.

Motorists, cyclists, backpackers, and many whose motives remain unknown visit the park to the tune of 2,250,000 each year. Traffic, trail erosion, competition for backcountry and developed campsites, and other problems have replaced the cares of daily living that dominated here in pre-park years. Shenandoah, once home to a few hardy mountain people, has become a microcosm of the difficulties shared by parks and wild areas everywhere. The dilemma park managers share is that of balancing preservation and use, and their policy, now slowly evolving, is that of favoring preservation. Shenandoah, as a consequence, may someday follow areas less resistant to human impact in limiting the number of backcountry visitors. Or, in keeping with future trends, visitors to all wild areas, this one included, may find themselves paying fees for such "nonconsumptive" uses as day hiking, rock climbing, birding, and nature photography. Just as campers and hunters now pay fees, so also may we all.

Whether limitations, fees, and other tools of management are incompatible with backcountry experience depends on an understanding of that experience. The popularity of wilderness encounter in Shenandoah and elsewhere is a direct outgrowth of the post-industrial society in which we live. People no longer deal directly with the land as they did in the pre-industrial phase of American economic life, or with the products mined and harvested from the land as was more common in industrial society. Today people deal with people. Ours is a service-oriented society in which teachers, bureaucrats, students, managers, and professionals far outnumber those who produce food and material goods. Implicit in this situation are a host of difficulties. In dealing with people, those who are employed in service-oriented positions face the unpredictable facets of the individual human personality and the frustrations of bucking a highly institutionalized society. Rarely are the results of one's work seen as directly as they were when the harvest was in or the land had been worked. Life has become difficult in new ways.

One key result of this situation is the inability of individuals to identify meaningful goals and manipulate their environments toward achieving them. In the past seeds could be sown and corn would grow, but more modern equivalents, such as high grades in college and money in the bank, are no longer reliable guarantors of a career or a house in the suburbs—and in fact these may not be desirable goals for many. Even when goals are identified, the modern service-oriented employee/professional is not the manipulator of his environment, but rather is being increasingly manipulated by it.

The effects on society are many and diverse. Vast numbers of people, despairing of any hope that their individual efforts might somehow change their lives, their cities, or environments, have foresaken career, civic, and governmental responsibilities. Creative outlets for substantial numbers are increasingly found through manipulation of natural environments toward achievable goals. The new farms managed by young, dissatisfied social splinter groups are one such outlet. A very common manifestation of this need is the trend toward skill-oriented outdoor experience. Backpackers, rock climbers, kayakers—all those who find challenge in wild country—know that with skill their particular slices of nature can be manipulated with calculable predictability. In nature the pieces can be put together to form a whole. It is often for this reason that parks and wilderness areas are most vocally supported by the managers, teachers, students, and professionals in our society.

For park planners there are specific management policies implicit in this, the most pertinent here being that wilderness does not need to be primeval. Most backcountry users need only to know that the rules of nature and not those of man apply. For the skill-oriented user of wildlands, it is enough that one can be unconcerned with others and that only the problems and challenges of reading the weather, the rock, or the rapids need matter. Shenandoah National Park provides this kind of experience, even though most of the park is little more than forty-year-old second-growth forest. The same may also be said of reclaimed wild areas in the Blue Ridge from Catoctin Mountain Park in Maryland southward into the Chattahoochee National Forest in Georgia.

It is also suggested that the idea of wild corridors—that is, long, narrow belts of wildlands—be given greater priority. The Appalachian Trail is a prime example of this concept. Wilderness experience is psychological as much as physical, and for many, getting out of sight and sound of humanity for extended periods is satisfaction enough. Land should be purchased or placed under scenic easement restrictions along the portions of the Appalachian Trail not presently protected, and other similar trails should be developed. For those who prefer white water to hiking, riverways should be protected from instrusions. In all cases, these corridors should not be easily accessible to people whose motives and goals differ widely from the intended users. If backcountry is redefined and made available in light of these criteria, the overcrowding and environmental impact problems of parks such as Shenandoah can be greatly eased.

Always there is an exception. For some of us there is a definite need to know that we are deep within country that is untouched by man. Two federal agencies, the National Park Service and the U.S. Forest Service, administer most of the Blue Ridge lands currently being preserved. Under the Park Service are the Great Smoky Mountains and Shenandoah national parks, the Blue Ridge Parkway, Harpers Ferry National Historical Park, and Catoctin Mountain Park. The Forest Service, within the several national forests along the Blue Ridge, manages less extensive tracts strictly for preservation. Principally these are areas set aside under the provisions of the Wilderness Act of 1964. The Cohutta and Ellicott Rock wilderness areas in Georgia, the Joyce Kilmer–Slickrock, the Shining Rock, and Linville Gorge wilderness areas in North Carolina, and the James River Face Wilderness in Virginia have been set aside under the act and are administered by the Forest Service. Within the National Park Service lands are other designated wildernesses.

Mount Rogers National Recreation Area, Virginia, a Forest Service area with extensive backcountry, is managed primarily for recreation. Permits are required for entry into the Linville Gorge and Shining Rock wildernesses, with a further restriction on numbers of visitors in effect at Linville Gorge. State and private parks, while rarely embracing much primeval wilderness, occasionally contain some spectacular backcountry. Mount Mitchell State Park and Grandfather Mountain Park (privately owned) in North Carolina, and Gray-

71

son Highlands State Park in Virginia are outstanding examples. In short, enough untouched backcountry exists in the Blue Ridge to give almost anyone whatever sense of isolation and self-reliance he might need.

That Shenandoah National Park, together with the rest of the Blue Ridge in Virginia and Maryland, could be the object of so much use is an indication of that country's true character. In essence, the northern Blue Ridge is both a disappointment and a promise. The main spine of the Blue Ridge in these states is often less than two thousand feet above the Piedmont and Great Valley, but it is a very different sort of landscape from the low country. The ridges are heavily wooded, usually steep, and generally undeveloped. From access points at the gaps where roads cross, one can quickly disappear into country that has the look of wilderness. The various Appalachian Trail guides, maps, and trail markings define the route along the ridges, and the number of miles and minutes to the next gap are well known.

In short, the ridges are places that offer wilderness as you like it. There is no obligation to hike a set distance or even to hike at all. The rocky promontories that occasionally jut above the forest are ideal places just to sit, watch birds, or maybe "get high on mountains." In fact, the best use to which these mountains are put might be rock sitting. The rocks, of course, are only the beginning. Weather and setting must also be right. Take a clear, calm day with the temperatures in the sixties, add some warm, flat rocks in places where there is little chance of being disturbed, and the conditions are right for drowsing or napping. As vision fades, sounds drift in—birds, wind, or perhaps the far-off roar of a river. The mind wanders. The effect can be hypnotic. At the very least it is a luxury we well might allow ourselves more often.

Memory, it has been said, is not a function of time but of intensity of experience. Some of my most profound memories of the Blue Ridge have resulted from afternoons spent in solitude on high, rocky prominences. After a moment of contemplation, the sun and solitude are enough in themselves to suppress any urge to move on. The moments pass and the afternoon sun pulls long shadows from the surrounding forest. If the time is right, hazy purple dusk may settle into the hollows, leaving only the ridges burnished with bronze. Evening is melancholy on the ridges; it is a time of repose, blue distances, and flat layers of smoke hanging over farmhouses. To have stayed put this long is to be ready again for companionship and warmth. The time spent alone, perhaps more than anything else, has been a preparation that will be good until again there is solitude, a warm rock, and sunshine.

If such distant views from rocks are exceptional, it is the forest that makes them so. In these mountains one must have an appreciation for trees. Forests such as those in the Appalachians may seem oppressive to visitors from the western United States, but to anyone who has grown up in tree country they are a blessing. Like many who have always lived in the East, I take pleasure in hearing the wind gust through their leaves, feeling the coolness of shade, or perhaps smelling the odors so characteristic of some tree species. In a visual sense, trees have special meaning for me: sycamores for their bark patterns, beeches for their textural smoothness, maples for color, cedars for often looking twisted and gaunt, fir for their scent, and yellow poplars for flowers. The list is not a long one. I have definite preferences and know what to look for.

In Shenandoah it is the hemlocks to which I pay homage. In this I am perhaps little different from most people. The Appalachian deciduous forest is enhanced by its evergreens in the estimation of many. At Big Meadows, the Civilian Conservation Corps planted balsam firs in the 1930s. Now mature, these groves attract so many visitors that paths have been worn to them. But the hemlocks were not planted. They are survivors of the farming and lumbering era. At two places, where relic stands of ancient trees grow, the park has a special mood.

One is Camp Hoover, the location of a cabin built for President Herbert Hoover. No better place could have been chosen. Hidden at the base of the Blue Ridge, the cabin sits astride a point of land where the Rapidan River and Laurel Fork pour over mossy rocks to meet each other. Towering above the cabin and surrounding it on every side are the hemlocks. Their size overpowers the cabin, which is itself made unobtrusive by log construction. Hemlock needles cushion the ground everywhere, and dense shade tends to keep the forest floor clear of anything but moss. The streams and the wind sighing through the high boughs are the only sounds. The effect is one of utter seclusion.

A spring morning there was one of the best I spent in Shenandoah. A soft warm breeze caressed the trees, sunlight patterned the forest floor, and hummingbirds flashed silently through the great branches. For hours my children played along the mossy banks of Laurel Fork, while my wife walked and then sat drowsing in the sunshine. Springtime is perhaps the best of seasons here, and this was a day not to be improved upon.

We entered the second of the hemlock stands just at dusk. The largest in Shenandoah National Park, it is known as The Limberlost. Hundreds of visitors see it daily during the summer, hiking a short trail off the Skyline Drive, but at dusk on this September evening it was empty of people and full of silence. The great trees seemed to gather the darkness and suppress the few sounds we made. Our footsteps were lost on the dark, springy humus, and we talked in whispers. Deeper into the hemlocks we walked, pausing a moment to examine a luxuriant growth of orange fungi, and then finally stopping when the light grew too dim. Just at that moment an owl hooted his first call of the night from somewhere close by. The sound seemed to accentuate the silence and gloom. With a sudden feeling of having seen enough, we turned and left.

Solitude of this sort is easy to come by in the northern Blue Ridge. The ridges are accessible to East Coast cities, yet they are just rugged enough to keep the motorist in his car and leave long sections of trails to the backpackers. Usually only a few renowned scenic spots are crowded with sightseers. Parking lots, interpretive signs, and graded trails are prerequisites for most occasional visitors to wilderness. The person in search of solitude needs only to seek out those long sections of ridge where there are no roads. There the sounds of traffic and voices give way to those of squirrels bounding through dry leaves or crows calling in the distance. The differences are abrupt and absolutely dependable.

Less expected than solitude, perhaps, is another seldom considered aspect of Shenandoah: climatic change with elevation. In the Rockies it is easily seen and always taken for granted. Even in the northern Appalachians it comes as no surprise because of the widely reported climatic extremes and definite tree line on Mount Washington, New Hampshire. Southward, heavy forest and tendencies toward warm days even in midwinter can cause visitors to forget the ferocity of winter on these mountains.

At five o'clock on a windy November afternoon I stood on the edge of 4049-foot Hawksbill Mountain in Shenandoah, feeling the cold air rip into my body. In the valley the day had been warm. This was unexpected. "Most people die of hypothermia at temperatures between thirty and fifty degrees Fahrenheit,"

Art Graham, Chief of Ranger Activities at the National Park Service Regional Office in Atlanta, later told me. The temperature then was about thirty-seven degrees Fahrenheit, with the wind-chill factor creating a still-air equivalent temperature far below that. Within minutes I was shivering uncontrollably, but the changing patterns of light cast by the setting sun were providing opportunities for beautiful photos.

"There are two stages in hypothermia." Graham continued. "The first we call 'exposure and exhaustion.' In it, the body loses heat faster than it is producing it. To create more heat, you shiver. But shivering eats up a tremendous amount of energy. It can't be kept up for long."

I shivered for perhaps twenty minutes, gradually becoming so overwhelmed by the process that I had difficulty manipulating my camera equipment. Another visitor walked up and managed an epithet about the wind. My lips wouldn't move, and my words weren't forming correctly when I talked with him. He left, too concerned about the cold to stay.

"In the second stage," Graham told me, "your energy is drained. Speech is slurred and you can't hold on to things. Finally you stop shivering for no logical reason. Shivering is a danger sign, but when you stop shivering—beware. You are dying."

I was alone on the escarpment now and the light was beginning to fade. Inexplicably, I no longer felt cold, but I could see no reason to stay longer. It is automatic with me. When the light fails, I always leave. Without further hesitation, I walked down the path and headed for my car. Off the top of the ridge, the wind lost its strength, and I began to warm from the exercise of the return walk. Unknowingly, I had brushed the second stage of hypothermia.

"When the shivering stops," the ranger said, "the cold reaches your brain. And that's usually the end. Reason gives way to fantasy. We've rescued people in that stage of hypothermia, and they've later told us they felt warm. The thing about hypothermia is that it's *not* a bad way to die. You can literally be dead before you know it."

I thought it over for a minute, only then realizing the way events had been leading me that evening on Hawksbill. Picking up on the pause, Graham finished.

"It's not unusual to find victims stark naked, frozen stiff in the snowdrifts. In the last stages they actually think they're hot. They just take off their clothes, lie down, and die."

"Their faces—how do they look?" I asked him, wondering how such a peaceful death might appear.

"Satisfied. Sometimes almost happy."

If climatic change with elevation works insidiously on the body, it is obvious in its effects on vegetation. Several times I have seen snow and rime in the Great Smoky Mountains National Park while attending the annual wildflower pilgrimage in Gatlinburg, Tennessee, in late April. Below, at elevations of as high as three thousand feet, the forest floor was carpeted with fringed phacelia, trilliums, showy orchis, phlox, jack-in-the-pulpits, and dozens of other wildflowers. Driving down the mountains meant passing through forests with bare branches, buds, and finally partially open leaves, and seeing the new season in it entirely passing within a half hour.

In its natural aspects the Blue Ridge of northern Virginia and Maryland differs little from the southern extremities of the range. The marked change is that of the cultural aspects of the region. Just below the Potomac River comes a quickening sense that this is not the South. In Maryland the feeling is confirmed. In response to the Germanic ancestry there, the architecture changes dramatically. This is Middle Atlantic architecture, with row-house styles and building configurations rarely used in the South. Only in a few places, mostly on the slopes of the ridges, are there remnants of Scotch-Irish architecture. Maryland's Pleasant and Middletown valleys are prime examples of the dominant styles. Little that is southern shows in the big barns and stone mills of the countryside, or in the Lutheran churches and high, narrow brick houses in the towns. Almost, but not quite, this is Pennsylvania Dutch country.

In a nation so caught up in change, it seems rather impossible that the cultural inheritance of the eighteenth and nineteenth centuries so strongly influences the mood of the land. But there is no doubt that it does. To me, the cultural South ends at the Potomac, a situation that creates a visual incongruity inconsistent with popular preconceptions about the Blue Ridge Mountains being home only to Scotch-Irish mountaineers. Perhaps the strongest confirmation of this change came at twilight on a cold, infinitely clear winter evening along the main street of Harpers Ferry, West Virginia, a town made more typical of Maryland by its industrial heritage. Across the Potomac, the Maryland Blue Ridge, here known as Elk Ridge, loomed snow-covered and silent above the town. Close at hand, the street was empty of people; only an occasional car crunching across the snow created movement. The houses and shops, characteristically right next to the street, were silhouetted against the deep blue of last light. As I walked the empty sidewalk, the shapes suddenly looked foreign—European, not American. Holland, was it? Or Germany? I wasn't sure. Perhaps it was the darkness. At that moment only the shapes showed, creating the impression that I was far from the Blue Ridge and even farther from the South. The mountains and their people had again betrayed their ability to transform themselves to other times and other places.

In getting to know the people of the northern remnants of the Blue Ridge, one is instantly impressed with the fact that the mountains are not important influences in their lives. Exceptions exist, of course, but generally the older people here are governed by traditions shared elsewhere to an equal extent. More so than anywhere else along the range, urban influences are felt here. Washington and Baltimore with their millions are each only fifty miles from the easternmost ridges. Thousands of people commute that far to work each day, filling the coaches of the AMTRAK *Blue Ridge* each morning and evening or leaving dozens of cars at carpool meeting points along the roads. Spending three hours each day in a train or car is utter folly, but the alternative—life in the city—is for many an even worse fate. Energy costs rise, and commuting to the country grows more impractical, but the demand continues for homes in the hills.

Property values, especially in the mountains, have become grossly inflated, bringing at least one result that can be commended. Old houses, once thought to be worthless, are now being carefully restored. To live in a log house two centuries old, for example, was once so socially undesirable that most of them were covered with cheap siding. Now a log-cabin chic is evident. The siding has been stripped off—often at great expense—and the mortar is replaced, the chimneys are repaired, and the new owners are among the proudest in the hills. Realtors, when they are lucky enough to list livable mountain houses and property, can expect to be deluged with prospective buyers. Even houses beyond easy restoration are of such value now that trained housewrights—craftsmen skilled in restoring log houses—are again in demand.

Exploring in the Maryland Blue Ridge one late summer evening, I happened on a back road where the houses, now mostly covered with various styles of siding, were obviously of one basic design. Most probably a Scotch-Irish immigrant group had chosen this place because it is high, almost level, and close to a spring. The spring, indicated on my Appalachian Trail map, was the reason I was on the road. When I finally found it, I also located a lovingly restored log cabin.

"Is the water safe to drink?" I asked a lady who emerged from the cabin.

"Certainly," she replied. "Everyone around here uses the spring for drinking water."

As we talked, a story unfolded that was both typical and unique. She was a teacher just about to retire from employment in Washington, D.C. Looking for a place in the country in early 1975, she'd put ads in two local newspapers, offering twenty thousand dollars cash for a country house. The ad was seen by the couple who had restored the cabin and for whom a move had become imperative. Could they actually get twenty thousand dollars for their old cabin, the owners had wondered. They could, and they did. Moreover, they could have sold it for thirty-five thousand dollars, based on similar sales along the Blue Ridge in the vicinity.

"Would you like to see the inside?" my new acquaintance asked. I accepted and we proceeded toward the back door. "One thing," she cautioned as she reached to open the door. "Don't be frightened by Stonewall. He won't hurt you."

Before I could respond, the door flew back and a huge white English bulldog, complete with studded collar, barreled toward me, whuffing and snuffing as he came. "Sixty-nine pounds, he weighs," she proclaimed as he checked me out. She had a right to brag. The dog was pure beef—and friendly to the point of over-enthusiasm.

The cabin itself was typical of those built about two hundred years ago. The entire ground floor was a single rectangular room with a fireplace at one end. A steep, narrow staircase led to the second floor, which consisted of two small rooms. There just wasn't much to the old cabins, but what they lacked in space they made up in sturdiness. Walls were constructed from carefully hewn logs that were notched at the ends to fit tightly at the corners. Chimneys were usually quite massive and were made with flat stones picked up on the farmer's land and then plastered together with thick southern clay. The roofs were originally made from oak shakes and later were often covered with tin, and floors, when they existed, were likely of yellow poplar.

The cabins were dark, smoky places with low beams and the smell of countless hearth fires. Cooking was done in iron pots hung over the fire, food was prepared on the table, and beds were jammed close together on the second floor. Most of the farmer's work was done outdoors; perhaps only that made the lack of space in the mountaineer cabins tolerable. By today's standards, a building of such small size would not be taken seriously as a permanent home. Typically, then, this cabin had been enlarged during its restoration. Two more small rooms had been added on the ground floor, one a lavatory and the other a bedroom. The former owners had done a good job; the cabin was a bargain. In all, the situation was much like that in which many old houses have been restored along the length of the Blue Ridge. Only the price differed.

At one time there was probably less wildness left in the Blue Ridge from the location of Shenandoah National Park northward than anywhere else in these mountains. But in the past fifty years the return of the land to nature has been profound. It is the overriding characteristic of the countryside—the one sweeping statement that most characterizes the situation on these ridges. Until the 1930s man needed the timber and the soil. Charcoal and lumber, crops and pasture were the land's best contribution to man. Today the cash crops come from elsewhere. Aesthetic rewards are the bounty of the hills now. A hike in the backcountry, a climb on Stony Man, or maybe a ridge behind some homes in outer suburbia: this is the Blue Ridge from Shenandoah north. Whatever else this country is, it's high, it has trees, and it is good for people.

Color Plates 51–74

51 Dawn from Mount Le Conte, Great Smoky Mountains National Park.

52 Fraser firs on Clingmans Dome.

53 Shenandoah National Park from Hawksbill Mountain.

54–58 Appalachian arts and crafts. Carvings created by the hands of Ben Bar of Habersham County, Georgia, an apple doll and quilts on display in Tallulah Falls, Georgia, and apple butter steaming at West Virginia's Mountain Heritage Arts and Crafts Festival.

59 Big Meadows, Shenandoah National Park.

60 Mountain laurel on a Maryland cliff.

61 Laurel Fork at Hoover Camp, Shenandoah National Park.

62 Floodplain pool along the Shenandoah River in West Virginia.

63 The Shenandoah from Keyes Gap, West Virginia.

64 Gathering speed in the dusk, the waters of the Shenandoah approach the Blue Ridge at Harpers Ferry, West Virginia.

65 *Cladonia* lichens fringed with frost.

66 The Shenandoah at the Blue Ridge.

67 Sculptures in ice at a fall.

68 Leaves sheathed in ice at a Maryland waterfall.

69 Harpers Ferry and the Shenandoah (upper left) and Potomac rivers.

70 A johnboat awash along the bank of the Shenandoah.

71 Mirror smooth, the Potomac pauses before turning to white water at the Blue Ridge.

72 The Potomac, interlaced with islands, from Maryland Heights, Maryland.

73 Maryland Heights at Harpers Ferry.

74 Moonrise, the mountains, and a fisherman's fire along the Potomac.

54

56

55

57

58

59

60

61

65

66

64

69

70

71

The Passage of the Potomac

The evening sun was etching sharp shadows into the cliffs above the Virginia side of the Potomac River when the vultures appeared. Without a sound, their wings motionless, every one in perfect position, they hung in the still air. Then, as if by command, the flock wheeled in unison—a perfect maneuver that brought them out over the river. From where I stood, high on the Maryland side of the Potomac, I could see every movement. Their heads were visible now, red and ugly for birds of such grace. Forty-six vultures, I counted them, and still not a wing moved. Closing fast, they soared overhead, looking like waves of World War II bombers, and disappeared silently over the ridge above me.

Vultures frequent the cliffs where the Potomac and Shenandoah rivers join to cut through the Blue Ridge at Harpers Ferry, West Virginia. In winter hundreds of them, predominantly turkey vultures, but also a few blacks, can be seen riding the currents created by winds hitting the slopes. With the coming of spring, ospreys join them in spiraling the updrafts. Then, during the summer, they disperse to nest, only to return as the days shorten into autumn.

When it is understood that vultures are birds of little energy, their affinity for the Potomac Water Gap is readily apparent. The cliffs provide safe places where they may lay their eggs, launch themselves into space, or sit serenely. Early morning finds them hunched by the dozens in trees along the Appalachian Trail and riverbank, waiting for the sun to create rising air currents. Old trees, protected on National Park Service land, serve as convenient roosts, and carrion is plentiful along the highways in the area. Under such favorable conditions, the great birds can outlive humans. In fact, their life-span may approach a century. People come and go, but the vultures have it all worked out. The place belongs to them.

There is a certain spectral quality to these birds that befits this country. They add mood and help impart the touch of eloquence that is first in evidence here as one drives up from the metropolitan areas to the east. Thomas Jefferson overstated it a bit in 1781 when he wrote that this place was "worth a voyage across the Atlantic." Nevertheless, the Potomac and Shenandoah rivers are fast and powerful, and the Blue Ridge crowds in over them until they are squeezed into one swift and sometimes dangerous passage. Precipitous cliffs of gray and black shale rim the rivers, the waters narrow, the roads and houses are squeezed in, and history is so telescoped that two hundred years of this nation's reminiscences can be seen at a glance.

Of the three major rivers that breach the Blue Ridge to flow eastward toward the Atlantic, the Potomac is the most powerful. Rising in the Allegheny Mountains four hundred miles from its estuary, it flows through the Ridge and Valley geologic province to confront the Blue Ridge in a direct manner. By the time the river reaches Harpers Ferry, it is more than seven hundred and fifty feet in width and flowing at a rate of 9263 cubic feet per second. The Shenandoah, on the other hand, is a creature of the valley for which it is named. Rising in the foothills to the southwest, it stays within the confines of the Shenandoah Valley for a hundred and fifty miles, hugging the Blue Ridge most of the way. A major river in itself, the Shenandoah is broad, powerful, and fully worthy of the poetry and song that has given it so special a place in American history.

When the two rivers approach their confrontation with the mountains at Harpers Ferry, their character changes. Sluggish meanders give way to straight chutes of swift water as the ancient upthrust shales of the Blue Ridge provoke them. White-water stretches, familiar to rafters, canoeists, and kayakers, and bearing such names as Bull Falls, The Staircase, and Whitehorse Rapids, rear up on the course of the rivers. When the rivers are at normal flow or slightly above it, the white waters are the sort of challenge popular with Class III canoeists and kayakers. But at flood stage they become torrents impossible to navigate.

When the rivers are in flood, as they are each year, the quantity and power of their flow in this constricted place is nothing short of awesome. No flood-control dams impound either river, and when nature wills it, the floods passing through the Potomac Water Gap are just as ferocious as they always have been. At normal average flow, the Potomac at the Blue Ridge is rocky and island-studded. Fishermen jump from rock to rock, seeking out the deep runs where catfish forage. Canoeists and kayakers manage well, though rescues are sometimes necessary even in low water.

In flood, the rocks are so far submerged that reading their locations on the surface of the heaving, roiling river is impossible. Two or three days after the soil is saturated with rain, the Potomac and Shenandoah begin quick rises. Huge sycamores, rafts of debris, and the flotsam of civilization tumble downriver. The increase in the Potomac's flow in flood is fantastic. At 11:30 p.m. on the night of June 23, 1972 (during

Hurricane Agnes), the river was pouring 347,000 cubic feet of water per second through the Blue Ridge—roughly thirty-seven and a half times its normal average flow. On March 19, 1936, a maximum flow of 480,000 cubic feet per second (fifty-two times normal and the greatest since record keeping began) passed the same spot.

Confined to roughly its normal channel by the cliffs of the Blue Ridge, the Potomac produced a tremendous surge. The ground seemed to tremble, the damp air reeked with the smell of mud, and the very sight of the river so suggested power that standing near it was somehow a matter of pure nerve. In those great floods the Potomac was sending the same volume of water through an eleven-hundred-foot-wide passage that the Mississippi River, ranging between one half and one mile in width, pushes past the vicinity of Memphis, Tennessee, under average conditions.

With the passing seasons, the rivers and their effects on the land change in sometimes profound ways. Winter is the season when the water is at its most beautiful. Cold and often clear, the Shenandoah takes on the blue-green look so characteristic of rivers rising in limestone country. The Potomac, in its turn, becomes milky blue. With the rains of late winter and early spring, sediment pouring seaward turns both rivers a frothy brown. Summer and autumn find the waters warm, filled with microorganisms, and brownish yellow. As the water warms and cools in response to the seasons, it affects the layers of air resting above it on clear, still nights. If the humidity is high, fog follows the river courses, and spiraling columns of warm, moist air rise skyward from the water. Within an hour of sunrise the fog is usually gone, but before it leaves, the water gap is a place of misty moods and white water dancing into indeterminate distances.

They are an inseparable part of the Blue Ridge, these rivers, if only because they speak so eloquently of the vast quantities of water that fall in the Southern Appalachians. Forty inches of precipitation is the yearly average, with more than twice that falling in some places—the Smokies, for example, where more rain and snow fall than anywhere else in the continental United States except the Pacific Northwest. The effect, whether it is on rivers like the Chattahoochee in Georgia, the New in North Carolina and Virginia, or the Potomac, is the same. Tiny cascades gather on countless hills and drop quickly to form what the southerner calls branches or runs. These in turn become creeks and then rivers. Flowing swiftly down shoals or rapids, they drain to the Gulf of Mexico and the Atlantic.

But not all the water finds its way into the rivers. The lush, all-pervading forests of the Blue Ridge trap much of the water that reaches the land. In the summer the trees return that water to the atmosphere through transpiration. So great is the volume of water reaching the atmosphere in this way that it adds significantly to the blue haze that gives these mountains their name. Standing alongside a creek in north Georgia several years ago, I discussed this relationship between forests and stream flow with a group of conservationists. Fifty years ago, several remembered, the rivers flowing off the Georgia Piedmont were larger than they are today. We argued that everything seems bigger when one is younger. But no, they insisted, the rivers were broader and deeper. When it was remembered that the Piedmont was deforested in those years to make room for cotton, there could be but one conclusion. With little vegetation to compete for surface water, the rivers were actually larger—and a great deal muddier—than today.

But all this is perhaps too general. These days most rivers are of more interest for their white-water boating qualities. River running is a sport that must be experienced to be appreciated. Long ago I learned that standing beside rivers does little to help one appreciate their power and subtleties. Lying down and looking across at water level is better, but getting on, or in, a river brings the only meaningful identification. Before I had been on the Shenandoah, I failed to understand the willingness to endure pain that I saw in a powerfully built young man who had knelt too long in a C-1 covered canoe on that river. Perhaps hours ago the circulation had gone out of his cramped legs, but he had gone on. And I wondered why so many people would risk death on the Chattooga as I watched its mountain-clear waters slide past at Earl's Ford on the Georgia–South Carolina line. Does a man need to offer himself up to whatever dare might have been written into the pages of a novel?

Then, after my first white-water trip, I began to understand. Death is not always tempted for profound reasons. Though a dare may be enough, it is only the least of motives. White water is a medium in which everything is compressed and speeded, and concentration must be total. For the river runner, that unique quality alone is often enough. And there is the flash of fear I felt when I first came to grips with the power of the Potomac. River running is an emotional experience. If having been taken by a river can be turned, through practice, into one of taking rivers, there is little an individual won't do to find and challenge new white water. Rivers become a mélange of beauty, emotion, physical endurance, mental challenge, and, most of all, deception. It is well to remember one generality: deception is the art developed to a high degree by most rivers. Water, reaching over rocks, does the unexpected. It veers, it leaps, it sucks and swirls—it is a thing of beauty and power, absolute and impartial in its judgment. Only in the knowledge of this can a boater be safe—and then never quite safe. Reading rivers, like understanding rock faces, is a skill with high stakes. In common with all wilderness skill sports, river running becomes a medium in which we define challenges and put ourselves to the test. And in some measure define ourselves.

Almost twelve hundred feet above the point where the Potomac and Shenandoah rivers meet, the ridges level out. The forest here is second-growth, but it is well along toward maturity, and it forms a satisfactory shield for the Appalachian Trail, which crosses the Potomac on its way to Maine or Georgia. On days when the air is clear, I climb. Mountains tumbling across long horizons and ridges etched sharply against the sky are a part of me not readily denied for long. Not high, not remote, the ridges are most to my liking when few others venture on them. Winter is my time on these heights.

In the cold stillness of a morning after eight inches of fresh powder snow had fallen, I left the rivers and started up the ridge on the West Virginia side of the Potomac. Reluctant at first to corrupt the unblemished snow with my footprints, I hesitated. Low clouds, drifting just over the ridgetop, thinned as I stood there, letting sunlight sweep in patches through a stand of hemlocks in front of me. Except for the roar of the rivers, there were no natural sounds. Nothing moved. Then the wind began to trouble the snow-laden hemlocks. It is always the same in the stillness of such mornings. No more than the tips of a few boughs may be wind-touched at first, but it is enough to begin the snow music. Beneath the smooth curve of the snow on the needles, a tree moves and a spray of snow crystals shatters into the sunlight. A symphony has begun. More branches and other trees respond to the quickening tempo of the wind, and the air is filled with snow crystals, each an infinitesimal supernova—a flashing image of its mother star. Veils and streamers dance in the sunlight as the powder catapults and collapses from the hemlocks. For a few fantastic minutes the air is filled with snow music. Then all is over. The hemlocks are unburdened and the wind blows freely through them. Without a sound, the music is ended.

I never reached the ridgetop that morning. The snow and sunlight consumed my interest, leaving me little time to move on. Not far from the hemlocks, a small creek runs down the ridge, splashing over a series of ledges. In the night, ice draperies had sheathed each small waterfall, encasing leather-brown oak leaves in transparent armor and creating random shapes where water had spattered against sticks and rocks. Globular mounds of ice competed with miniature gargoyles for sculptural effect. The rich colors of the wet leaves reflected in the ice, tinting the clear sheathing with russet brown. At a larger waterfall such small fantasies might never have been noticed. Here they commanded the attention—became the artistic ultimate of the place. In one respect the morning had been typical: I seldom reach my intended destinations.

Like many a hiker, I tend to stop occasionally on Maryland Heights, a prominence from which there is an excellent view of both the Potomac-Shenandoah confluence and the town of Harpers Ferry. On almost any weekend a few rock climbers, backpackers, and day hikers can be seen working their way up the cliffs or along a spur of the Appalachian Trail. Only when the hour is late or the weather turns cold is the place at all lonely. At those times it is, in a sense, a ghostly place, whispering with the sounds of the Union or Confederate sentries who once watched the town below.

Almost at dark one winter evening I stood at the cliff edge on the Heights. The wind blew strong through a cedar with a hiss like escaping steam, preventing me from hearing even the rivers. At that moment the sound of a fife came up through the wind with complete clarity. The melody was southern, a song for Johnny Reb, but there was no one to be seen below. Glancing back to some rocks in front of me, my gaze met squarely the year "1863" chiseled so clearly in the stone that it could have been carved that afternoon. The fife stopped, the wind quickened in the gathering dusk, and I shivered.

For almost two hundred and twenty-five years the Potomac Water Gap has figured in the American experience. Jefferson saw it as a place of natural wonder and beauty, the military located an arsenal there, and

John Brown and his sons met their end in a firehouse near the arsenal. Devastated by war and floods, the town of Harpers Ferry eventually shriveled to a remnant of its former self. Then, in the 1950s, restoration began. Today the gap is the location of Harpers Ferry National Historical Park. That so much happened is a direct result of the presence of the rivers. Men came, built their town and factories, channeled the water into canals, and then watched as almost everything was destroyed by the floods. Today it is the same; the rivers still can take their toll. Occasionally one sees that fact in the countenance of the people.

If it had not been for the rivers, the woman I met on a street that ends near the Shenandoah would not have been more than a passing acquaintance. With me was my son, and the two of us had stopped when the man sitting with her on the porch of a modest house gave a friendly hello. I talked with him about nothing in particular for a few minutes. The conversation seemed at an end and the woman had said nothing, yet I knew she was watching my boy. We had just turned to leave when she finally stood up and came to the steps.

"He has beautiful hair," she said, not taking her eyes off him. Something in her voice made me look closely at her. "My boys had beautiful hair too. One of them had red hair just like that." I sensed she was talking only to keep us there, and so we stood, saying nothing for a minute before I again turned to leave.

"They're gone," she said. "The river took them. My boys." She walked slowly back to her chair and stopped. "You take good care of him. Watch him."

"I will," I said, and we continued our walk.

"That must have been ten years ago when they drowned," my neighbor later told me. "Cutest little boys you ever saw. One had black hair and the other red, like Bill's. They stopped by here on their way to the river. I believe they had fishing poles. Oftentimes they'd stop by." She looked away.

"It was tragic," she finally said. "Just pure tragic."

Misty moods, deceit, death. Nature does not distinguish between them. She only admits to the possibility. People still live with that.

Headquartered in an old movie theater high above the rivers is the Appalachian Trail Conference, the coordinating agency for the sixty-two regional clubs which maintain this footpath as it follows the length of the Blue Ridge and continues on into New England. Talking with Les Holmes, retired director of the Conference, one slowly gains some insight into the mystique that surrounds this, the oldest and longest continuously marked footpath in the world. The trail, initially completed in 1937, survives and succeeds because individuals have devoted themselves to it. Over the years the trail has gained a cadre of hikers who defend its interest and maintain it in the face of increasing use and encroaching development.

The trail's history is one of repeated rescue by individuals, especially during the formative years, followed by the solving of tremendous logistical problems. In locating the trail north from the Great Smokies to the Peaks of Otter in the 1930s, members had to decide on a two-hundred-mile route through territory about which there was no public information at all. Adequate topographical maps did not even exist. All that was known was that the Blue Ridge main crest divides in the region into two forks which form an immense oval with as much as fifty miles of elevated valleys between the high eastern and western ranges. Nobody knew the mountains but the people of the hills, and it was one of them who finally outlined the route. Over the years there always seemed to be someone who could rescue a project or manage a program. Walking the Appalachian Trail today is possible only because the work of the faithful made it so. Whatever mystique the trail has is justly deserved.

Since 1968 federal funds have been authorized to help finance purchase of private lands through which the trail runs. Purchasing is being done by most of the involved states with the aid of matching funds from the federal Bureau of Outdoor Recreation. Routine maintenance of the 2036-mile trail and its 238 shelters is accomplished by volunteers. Trail repairs are often a matter of personal dedication of the sort shown by L. D. Gastiger, an elderly property owner in the rugged and spectacular Laurel Fork Gorge near Boone, North Carolina. When the Appalachian Trail Conference first sought permission to route the trail through his property, there was only bitter opposition on his part. Retired and in his eighties, he'd taken the 309-acre tract from a logging railroad in lieu of a pension, and now he wanted to be left alone with it. The gorge had everything: giant hemlocks, a stream and forty-foot falls, a three-hundred-foot cliff, and natural pinnacles. But the old man was at first adamant; no trail. Only with time and gentle persuasion was permission finally secured to put the trail through the gorge.

When the trail clearing began, the old man stood by, watching dubiously. "Could you tell us where to route the trail?" someone asked. He supposed so, and he did. The advice was good, the crew followed it, and the old man began taking an interest in "his" section of trail. When wooden bridges washed out, he repaired them, even obtaining a junked truck frame with which he made a washout-proof bridge. Shortly before his death, he sold the Laurel Gorge property to the Appalachian Trail Conference. Today it is one of the most beautiful places on the entire trail.

These days the Trail Conference keeps tabs on the number of users by methods which even include electronic sensors placed deep in the woods, and in the process has noted that use has more than doubled since 1970 to some four and a half million hikers who used the trail for some distance in 1974. Two trail sections within the scope of this book—Great Smoky Mountains and Shenandoah national parks—place first and third in numbers of users per year, while the White Mountains National Forest in New Hampshire ranks second.

Under such impact, the trail and the quality of experience of those using it suffer in some places. But by and large, the hikers come into the Trail Conference headquarters with stories that differ little from those of their predecessors. If there is any difference, it is a naïveté that betrays the number of novices using the trail. Perhaps typical was the couple whose lunch in a Shenandoah National Park cabin owned by an affiliate trail club was interrupted by a skunk. When the skunk walked in the open front door looking for food, the woman swished it with a broom—with results anyone familiar with skunks might have expected. When the main room became unbearable, the couple retreated into the bedroom to eat, leaving that door open. The skunk followed, again received a swish, and again made its reply. When the couple turned the cabin keys in to the club, they complained about paying rental, insisting that the cabin smelled too much.

Animal stories are the favorites told by hikers, with bear stories perhaps ranking first in the lore. Anyone who has hiked the trail sooner or later meets a bear, feels exhilarated about the encounter, and details the experience to others. Occasionally an unusual story reaches the Appalachian Trail Conference offices. A complaint from a girl who was attacked by a raven seemed extraordinary enough to follow up. The resulting check revealed that the girl had been practicing bird calls at the time and had undoubtedly communicated with the raven. The most dangerous—and most rare—encounter involved a snake which sought out an occupied sleeping bag for warmth. The young man in the bag was almost awake in the morning when he felt the snake beginning to crawl in. Not knowing whether or not it might be poisonous, he lay still; then on the outside of the bag he pressed his extended arm down, isolating the snake. Then, sitting up slowly and keeping his hand and arm on the bag, he eased out and jumped clear. With a companion, he shook the bag. Out dropped a copperhead.

Such stories, however commonplace, amusing, or exciting, reveal less about the trail than the ways in which they are told. To the hikers who lived them, they are the high points that make everyday life more worthwhile. For countless individuals, the Appalachian Trail has been *the* place to go—a known quantity to which people who otherwise might never have experienced the joys of hiking have turned. Beyond the Blue Ridge are other, newer trails which owe their inspiration to this one: the Pacific Crest Trail has in recent years become a western counterpart in some ways, and on the books are proposed pathways, such as the North Country Trail, the Allegheny Trail, and the Lewis and Clark Trail.

There is more to the Potomac and its meeting with the mountains now than the sounds and silences of fast-moving water and weathered rock. For a measure of time yet unknown, the past and present course of collective and individual human destinies are here too. On windless nights the passage of the Potomac and Shenandoah rivers through the Blue Ridge can be heard a mile or more away. Some nights the Potomac seems louder; at other times it is the Shenandoah. The Blue Ridge, clearly defined against the sky glow from Washington or capped in low clouds, rolls off into the distance like a great petrified wave. And so it has been since the dawn of antiquity. The newcomer is man, standing alone in the darkness and taking it all in. With the coming, meaning has been imparted; the objective has become subjective. But that is the great good fortune of man—to seek meaning in all that exists. The rivers and ridges, captive in his mind, are because of him more now than they were.

Epilogue: Night Train to Toccoa

Moonlight fell in moving, luminous patches on the interior of the dark rail passenger coach. Through the wide windows I watched as the South swept past. It was March and the trees were still bare, letting the moon through to the ground and setting the tombstones, every one of them, aglow in a country cemetery. Lights and shadows moved by soundlessly, leaving a rich lode of impressions: stops in the small hours, steam hissing into the cold air, empty streets in towns medium and small, the pale glow of countless mercury vapor lamps. And above all, the hills, rounded and fringed with trees, but dark, always dark.

On such nights the Blue Ridge is a place of echoes and memories. Coon dogs and bear hounds yelping through the hollows and up ridges call ghosts from cabins that have long ago rotted beneath the greening forest. A thousand hearth fires leap to life, and every spirit is kin. In the frosty stillness the calendar is jumbled, the years are fused, and time means nothing. Mountaineers and campers share the same fires, and if they do not see one another, they might at least suspect a presence not of their own times. The train probed through the moonlit countryside and I watched, sensing that the night, which had begun so precisely and in so contemporary a manner, had lost itself in the years. If the dawn flight to Washington had been indicative of nature present and my own future, this night train trip offered glimpses of the southern past and intimations of my own place within it.

We left Washington's Union Station on schedule at 7:20 P.M. The train was the *Southern Crescent No. 1*, perhaps the best of the country's remaining fine trains. Four General Electric diesel E-8 engine units, an employees' car, a diner, a lounge car, sleeping cars, and coaches—three million pounds of steel—silver and burnished in the moonlight, made up the night's complement. Charlottesville, Lynchburg, Danville, Greensboro, Greenville, Atlanta, Birmingham, and New Orleans were on the schedule, with connections to the West Coast. Cities great and cities only vaguely familiar were listed. This was a crack passenger train—one of the breed that had survived the decline of railroad passenger service in the 1950s and 1960s and was there to greet the return to the rails on this night in 1976.

The moon was riding full over the Potomac as we moved across the trestle from the District of Columbia into northern Virginia. Public buildings, memorials, and monuments glowed warmly in floodlights, like great pearls set in the opalescence of moonrise. A panoply of lights reflected from the Potomac, and airliners, their underbellies cast in bronze by the ground lights, swung into Washington National Airport. It was incredible. Perhaps few sights in the world of man have ever equaled it.

Into Alexandria now, swift deceleration, eight doors opened simultaneously by porters, more passengers aboard, and then power, smooth and fast, as nearly ten thousand horsepower pulled the *Crescent* southward. In the diner I sat watching incredulously as a black waiter balanced a tray heaped high with plates of southern fried chicken, never missing a step while passengers bumped tables and each other and spilled coffee at a sudden dip in the rails. The place had a continuity with the past about it; the present was beginning to lack focus. The waiters, all very professional, could have been their fathers or grandfathers. Even the tables reflected the past. White linen and flowers, coffee-and-tea services from the 1930s, each pot and creamer burnished to a rich, lustrous patina by years of use, completed the setting. The time suddenly seemed decades wrong.

At length I retraced my way back through the quiet sleeping cars to the last coach, there to watch in the darkness as the Blue Ridge foothills slid by. Hours later, uncomfortable in the fitfulness of near sleep, I awoke fully. The car was completely dark. Forms were slumped or curled across seats, some wrapped in blankets, none moving. I walked to the rear of the car and stood facing out the back window. The rails spewed out into the moonlight from beneath the train like threads of silver. A freight train rocketed by from the other direction, unreeling itself blackly into nothingness. Turning, I walked the cars, not stopping until I reached the darkened diner. There was no one to be seen; everyone was down for the night. Coming back, I stopped in the club car and stood staring at a scenic photo on the wall. The car, cold and lifeless, was more comfortless than my own dark coach. I returned and curled up against the window to watch the farms, hills, and stars, until finally I fell asleep.

When the train rolled into Toccoa, in the hills of north Georgia, just at dawn, I thought back to a dawn on the runways of Atlanta's Hartsfield International Airport sixty miles to the southwest. The two trips were in a way symbolic. In them, the land and the past seemed linked in some seldom suspected but immutable bond. The land lay awakening on a fog-washed and still morning beneath the wings of an airliner, the past rode the rails at midnight, and together they filled the miles and years between. Sociologists have complained that there is no continuity with the past in America. But the land is the past, the people are the past, and in the Blue Ridge they have remained together. And that is the single greatest contribution of these mountains to modern America.

Places, those few that are left, where the people still touch the land, represent our last direct links with historical frontier America, its ways and thoughts. In these links and in the sense of continuity that men can derive from them, these places present possibilities for the present and future. Individuals make a nation, and a sense of perspective builds individuals. Continuity—one's roots, so to speak—and a feeling for what one can do with the world: these are the offerings of the Blue Ridge Mountains. They are what they can say to a person as a cultural and physical being. And in a collective sense, the mountains are the Southern Experience. They have given character and continuity to its people and in turn cannot be done without.

No one told me to climb the mountains. I climbed them myself, and I was glad. They offered me a sense of what they had been, of what I was, and what I could be. In some measure, the Blue Ridge is a part of me, and in like measure, it is all of us.

Photography

The Appalachians are not easily photographed. In the sense that a good mountain photograph must contain grandeur of the stereotype sort—with rocky peaks, snow fields, and deep blue sky—they are noncompetitive. And if a farm must have prospering herds, great barns, and golden fields of grain, they fail. Because so many photographers expect this subject matter from the region and try to force it, Appalachian photography has very often been a disappointment. In photographing these mountains, it is best to beware of such preconceptions.

Most of the time, the Appalachians seem impossible to photograph. A woolly haze cloaks the hills, and there are no strong compositional elements with which to work. Everything in the distance is rounded, subdued, and colorless, and in the forest close by, contrasty shadows doom color photography on many days. My way of circumventing this is to express the Blue Ridge as a mood. To me, this is melancholy country. In most places it is old, worn, and a little sad. The old farms and communities betray this, as do the abandoned fields and second-growth forests. The exceptions to this general mood are in those places that have escaped lumbering and cultivation. Parks and wilderness areas are prime examples. There, the mood is one of quiet grandeur—the grandeur of life. And of course, there is springtime, which in the Southern Appalachians is so much the best of seasons that it more or less revitalizes everything for a few weeks. Once a visual viewpoint is determined, subject matter becomes more readily apparent. The obviously good subjects are more readily distinguished from the bad. I further endeavor to deal with the timeless rather than the temporal. I look for patterns of man's passing and the return of nature.

Among the factors that determine the choice of a camera in landscape and historic sites photography, format is the most important. All things being equal, the best format for photography of this type is the largest the photographer can reasonably carry. With the completion of that statement, the qualifications begin. For reasons of time and finance, large-format work may not be practical. Perhaps the greatest qualifying factor, though, is the photographer. The minute a camera begins to interfere with making photographs, it is the wrong camera. Large-format equipment is so cumbersome to carry and time-consuming to set up that most photographers tend to pass up pictures rather than use it. For the vast majority the large format is thus entirely inappropriate.

Choose and use large-format equipment if (1) you do not let it sap your resolve and (2) you can afford it. If the choice is made in favor of large cameras, it will become obvious that using them is something of an addiction. Seeing the results and comparing them with small- or medium-format photographs of the same subject matter, one quickly realizes that there is still an important difference attributable to size alone. When the size advantage carries through into quality reproduction in a book or magazine, that edge is even more evident. Using the large equipment then becomes a privilege and a matter of pride; it is that which elevates the photographer in his profession and in his own self-esteem. When that point is reached, the equipment seldom limits the man using it.

With the cost of one color transparency in the 4″ × 5″ size being approximately ten times that of a 35mm slide and the expense of equipment being nearly proportionate, finance is yet another consideration. One must have a purpose in mind when expending money for large-format film and equipment. Unless there is an intention to publish or a personal need that demands large-format quality, the smaller cameras are quite adequate. At the very least, 35mm cameras give the photographer the opportunity to make a variety of photographs within the same time and money frame being utilized by a large-format worker in the same situation. I would therefore not ordinarily recommend 4 × 5 or even medium-format equipment to the casual photographer of landscape and historic sites.

My own equipment closely reflects the purposes to which it is put. For landscape and historic sites, I am presently using a 4 × 5 chosen for compactness. An elderly press camera, it is one of the smallest and most rugged ever made in its format. Stripped of its range finder and viewfinders, it can be used only for ground-glass work. Limited camera movements and short bellows extension restrict its versatility, but I understand the camera's limitations, know how to work within them, and can put it into action with speed engendered by years of practice. The key to technical quality in using it is the three modern high-quality lenses I possess. In focal lengths of 90, 254, and 135mm, they were made by the Ilex Optical Company and Schneider Optik. In appearance the outfit isn't much, but it fits in a small backpack and is probably one of the lightest and most compact 4 × 5 field outfits currently in use. The important point is that I have my equipment under control. With it I can go places and make images with comparative ease and reasonable versatility, in the process obtaining results that are technically indistinguishable from those expected with equipment bearing much greater prestige value.

Along with the 4 × 5, I also carry a 2¼″-square format camera which I use when I want to make second photos of subjects. The medium-format camera is also used for telephoto work with a 300mm lens or in situations where speed is critical. Extreme close-ups in the range of life size require the use of a 35mm camera and a macro lens. To photograph mosses, lichens, or the tiny and rare *Diamorpha cymosa* of the Georgia granite exposures, I have engaged in many hours of belly-down work right at ground level. In this type of photography especially, there is no substitute for actually looking through the camera. Seen from waist height, the world of miniature plants is nothing; seen from ground level through a camera viewfinder, it is everything.

Being there is the key to getting the photographs. More than anything else, the photographer must explore the world and keep his eyes open to its possibilities. Without that, the best equipment is nothing.

111

Parks and Recreation

For information about parks, wildernesses, and recreation activities, the following addresses will be helpful:

National Park Service areas
Great Smoky Mountains National Park, Gatlinburg, Tennessee 37738
The Blue Ridge Parkway, P. O. Box 7606, Asheville, North Carolina 28807
Shenandoah National Park, Luray, Virginia 22835
Harpers Ferry National Historical Park, P. O. Box 65, Harpers Ferry, West Virginia 25425
Catoctin Mountain Park, Thurmont, Maryland 21788

U.S. Forest Service areas (including southeastern national forests, wilderness areas, and recreation areas):
Southeast Forest Experiment Station, Post Office Building, P. O. Box 2750, Asheville, North Carolina 28802

State Parks
State of Georgia, Department of State Parks, 270 Washington Street, S.W., Atlanta, Georgia 30334
Stone Mountain Memorial Association, P. O. Box 778, Stone Mountain, Georgia 30083
North Carolina Travel and Promotion Division, Division of State Parks, Department of Natural and Economic Resources, Raleigh, North Carolina 27611
State of Virginia, Division of Parks, 1201 State Office Building, Richmond, Virginia 23219
West Virginia State Parks, State Capitol, Charleston, West Virginia 25305
Maryland Park Service, Tawes State Office Building, Annapolis, Maryland 21401

Privately owned park
Grandfather Mountain Park, Linville, North Carolina 28646

The Appalachian Trail
The Appalachian Trail Conference, P. O. Box 236, Harpers Ferry, West Virginia 25425

Selected References

Brooks, Maurice. *The Appalachians*. Boston: Houghton Mifflin, 1965.

Crandall, Hugh. *Shenandoah: The Story Behind the Scenery*. Las Vegas: K. C. Publications, 1975.

Dykeman, Wilma. *The French Broad*. New York: Holt, Rinehart and Winston, 1974.

Fisher, Ronald M. *The Appalachian Trail*. Washington, D.C.: The National Geographic Society, 1972.

Frome, Michael. *Strangers in High Places: The Story of the Great Smoky Mountains*. Garden City, N.Y.: Doubleday, 1966.

Garvey, Edward B. *Appalachian Hiker: Adventure of a Lifetime*. Oakton, Va.: Appalachian Books, 1971.

Kephart, Horace. *Our Southern Highlanders*. New York: Macmillan, 1933.

McVaugh, Rogers. "The Vegetation of the Granitic Flat-Rocks of the Southeastern United States." *Ecological Monographs* (April 1943) vol. 13, no. 2, 121–166.

Ogburn, Charlton. *The Southern Appalachians: A Wilderness Quest*. New York: William Morrow & Company, 1975.

Peattie, Roderick, ed. *The Great Smokies and the Blue Ridge*. New York: Vanguard Press, 1943.

Stupka, Arthur. *Great Smoky Mountains National Park*. Washington, D.C.: The National Park Service, 1960.

———. *Trees, Shrubs, and Woody Vines of Great Smoky Mountains National Park*. Knoxville, Tennessee: University of Tennessee Press, 1964.

———. *Wildflowers in Color*. New York: Harper & Row, 1965.

Thornbury, William D. *Regional Geomorphology of the United States*. New York: John Wiley & Sons, 1965.

Wigginton, Eliot, ed. *The Foxfire Book*. Garden City, N.Y.: Doubleday, 1972.

———, ed. *Foxfire 2*. Garden City, N.Y.: Anchor Press, 1973.

———, ed. *Foxfire 3*. Garden City, N.Y.: Anchor Press, 1975.